OLD CONTEMPTIBLE

Old Contemptible

by
HARRY BEAUMONT
of the
Queen's Own Royal West Kent Regiment

A PERSONAL NARRATIVE

EDITED AND INTRODUCED

BY

A. E. CLARK-KENNEDY

HUTCHINSON OF LONDON

HUTCHINSON & CO *(Publishers)* LTD
178–202 Great Portland Street, London W1

London Melbourne Sydney
Auckland Bombay Toronto
Johannesburg New York

First published 1967

*This book has been set in Baskerville, printed in Great Britain
on Antique Wove paper by Anchor Press, and
bound by Wm. Brendon, both of Tiptree, Essex*

To my many Belgian
friends who saved my
life and set me free

Contents

Illustrations

Acknowledgements

My first duty is to thank the author for the privilege of being allowed to edit his remarkable story, and Mrs M. Heath, of Wakering, Essex, for the photograph of her late husband, his dauntless companion during the greater part of his time as a fugitive in occupied Belgium. To the Princess Marie de Croy I am indebted for permission to make use of information which she put at my disposal, and facts related in her *War Memories* from which I also have leave to quote from Macmillan & Co.; and to Major Bushell, of the Queen's Bays, for providing facts relating to his own escape. The photograph of the group in the yard of the coal mine at Hornu-Wasmes was discovered in the possession of an old lady living in Frameries near Wasmes by M. Georges Licope, curator of the Musée de Centenaire in Mons, and is reproduced by his permission. To Brother Michael Appermans of Ekeren, formerly of the monastery at Averbode, I am indebted for an account of his own work in helping fugitive soldiers to escape; to the Mayor of Wasmes, and the Town Clerk, M. Fernand Roland, for putting me in touch with M. Robert Neusy, now living at Pessac, Gironde, and to the latter for kindly writing and confirming Beaumont's story of his stay at his father's house and sending us photographs of both his parents. Associated Book Publishers Ltd have given me permission to quote from *Condemned to Death* by the late Louise Thuliez, and Mrs George Bainbridge,

Methuen & Co., and the Macmillan Company of Canada to reproduce a verse from one of Rudyard Kipling's *Barrack Room Ballads*. The author himself would express his deep appreciation of the permission which the Old Contemptibles' Association have given him to use the name of their journal for the title of his book.

A. E. CLARK-KENNEDY

Cambridge

Introduction

by A. E. CLARK-KENNEDY

T HE 'old contemptible' hardly proved the kind of man
I had expected. Maybe old soldiers do 'never die', but this
one, at the age of eighty-two, with all his faculties intact,
showed no signs of even 'fading away'! His, too, was an
intelligent and determined face; his manner thoughtful and
collected; his whole make-up kind, careful and considerate.
Indeed, I was not surprised to learn that he had been a
bandsman and played the French horn; that he prided himself on his powers of observation and his retentive memory;
that he had been trained in the Army as a scout; that in spite
of his long service he had seen only three days' fighting in his
life! At least that is how Harry W. Beaumont, at one time a
private soldier in the Queen's Own Royal West Kent
Regiment, struck me as I sat with him in his semi-detached
house in south-east London where he had lived on alone
since his wife's death. And one thing was certain. A man of
few words, anything he said, any story he told, would be 'the
truth, the whole truth, and nothing but the truth'. And
nothing has happened since to alter this, my first impression
of him.

I had heard of him accidentally as one of the fugitive
soldiers Miss Cavell—to whom I had attempted to do
justice as the pioneer of modern nursing in Belgium and the

British patriot behind the German lines during the First World War—had hidden in her house. So I had immediately hastened down to see him. Her attempt to help him to escape, it is true, failed, as he himself relates. But this is not the reason why Beaumont is not mentioned in my book. I did not hear of him until after that had gone irretrievably to press![1]

'You were in the Army,' I said, 'when the war started?'

'Not exactly,' he replied, and proceeded to explain.

Born at Blean near Canterbury in 1884—his father tended stock on a farm—and brought up to no particular occupation, and jobs being short after the South African War, he had enlisted in the Royal West Kent Regiment in 1904 at the age of nineteen for a period of nine years, followed by three on the regular Reserve. So he was in civil life when the First World War began.

Beaumont had thoroughly enjoyed the Army, although it struck me that, by nature and temperament a conscientious man, he had probably been more abstemious than most soldiers. Posted to the 2nd Battalion of his regiment, his first station had been Hong Kong, which he remembers being wrecked by a typhoon, and whence he served for six months on the guard supplied to the British Legation at Pekin, and for a similar period with the garrison of the Treaty Port of Tientsin. Thence his battalion moved to Singapore, which he enjoyed the most of all his many stations. Then from Singapore they went to India. There they were stationed at Darjeeling, and then on the North-West Frontier at Peshawar.

He held his own in the boxing ring against all comers, weighing in at nine stone, and took pleasure in games of all kinds. As a marksman he wore the badge of one, crossed rifles, on his sleeve; also the star for distance-judging—range-

1. *Edith Cavell: Pioneer and Patriot* (Faber & Faber), London, 1965.

finders being then unknown. Nor did he neglect his educa-
tion. He succeeded in passing 'the first part of the first class
certificate'. This shows him to have been of above average
intelligence, and in consequence of which he was promoted
corporal. But he did not hold this rank for long. One night,
when acting orderly sergeant, he reported 'all present and
correct' when, as a matter of fact and as he knew, two of his
companions had not yet returned to barracks. In short, to
cover two pals he had risked his career. The pair were
arrested, and Corporal Beaumont was now in the orderly
room before his company commander with two choices open
to him only—a court martial or relegation to the ranks. He
opted for the latter, and became a bandsman, learning to
play the French horn with reasonable skill, he says, within
six months! In this capacity, too, he became a stretcher-
bearer, and was trained in first aid.

Nine years abroad without a break was understandably
long enough. Beaumont, like every soldier on foreign service,
hankered after home. Besides, he wanted to get married. So,
when his nine years in the Army expired in 1913, he did not
sign on for a further period of service, although, in accord-
ance with the terms of his original contract, he remained on
the regular Reserve, liable to be called up immediately in the
event of war. He was in the same position as Kipling's old
soldier of a slightly earlier date:

> 'I done my six years' service. 'Er Majesty sez:
> "Good-day—
> You'll please to come when you're rung for, an'
> 'ere's your 'ole back-pay."'

So Beaumont now came home, got work as an insurance
agent, the best job, as he put it to me, that he could get, and
settled down in 1913 to civilian and married life against the

background of the peace and prosperity of 'Edwardian' England. This idyll was to be quickly cut short. War was declared the following year, the Reserve was called up, and in duty bound he reported to his regimental depot at Maidstone. Beaumont, the old soldier, was 'Back to the Army again'.

> 'The sergeant arst no questions, but 'e winked the other eye,
> 'E sez to me, "Shun!" an' I shunted, the same as in days gone by;
> For 'e saw the set o' my shoulders, an' I couldn't 'elp 'oldin straight
> When me an' the other rookies come under the barrick gate.'[1]

No. 7555 Private Harry Beaumont was now posted to the 1st Battalion of his regiment, at that time stationed at the Curragh in Dublin, and events now started to move for all of them, whether serving soldiers or reservists, with startling rapidity. Within a fortnight he found himself on the high seas *en route* for France, his battalion part of the 13th Infantry Brigade of the Vth Division of the British Expeditionary Force under Lord French. They landed at Le Havre, where they entrained for the Landrecies. Thence the long march began to the blind collision with the oncoming German armies. There, too, his own story begins, related here as he wrote it down, now nearly forty years ago, with candour, simplicity and emotional detachment from events which in itself is truly remarkable. All that I have done is to add some information in my Introduction and Epilogue, and by way of footnotes, polish his manuscript, and revise it for the press, subtracting little and adding nothing. In short I have treated

---

1. Rudyard Kipling, *Barrack Room Ballads*, 1896.

his manuscript in exactly the same way as I would have treated my own draft of a book before handing it in to my publisher.[1]

Most of this information about Beaumont's life really came out later because, as can be imagined, when I first met him we started 'straight in' talking about the battle, his escape, and his wanderings. And, of course, I was particularly interested in his contact with Miss Cavell. So it is hardly to be wondered that I was soon pulling out my pen, preparatory to writing down much of what he told me.

'Don't bother!' he exclaimed. 'I'll give you my book to read. You'll find it all in that.'

'What, you've written a book?'

Whereupon Beaumont again proceeded to explain.

In about 1930, when there seemed to be almost an epidemic of people writing about their war experiences, he saw no reason why he should not try his hand at it too. So he wrote down an account of his adventures, got a friend to type it, and sent it to a publisher, who kept his manuscript for nine months, and then returned it to him, saying that he regretted he could not publish it because he was about to go bankrupt! And ever since this remarkable book had roosted unread in a cupboard, and was now produced for my inspection. I took it home. I read it from cover to cover. Then I went to sleep determined, and woke up more than ever determined, to get it published at all costs.

I had, of course, already discovered much, in the course of writing my life of Edith Cavell, about the remarkable organisation which grew up in Belgium and northern France to help British and Allied fugitives from Mons to get away. Indeed, I had already met and talked with the few surviving

1. His original manuscript has been deposited in the Imperial War Museum, Lambeth, London, S.E., with his forged identity card and the official notification of his death addressed to his wife by the War Office.

B

actors in it and with the sons and daughters of many of those deceased. Their stories fascinated me. For this was the first resistance movement of our distracted century, but one of which the British public, in the heat of the emotion engendered by the execution of a woman and a nurse, and under the clouds of war, remained at the time almost ignorant, and still remain largely unaware that it ever existed![1] They have heard of Miss Cavell, but of hardly anyone else connected with it, and many think, if they have heard of it, that Miss Cavell was the mainspring of it all. This is far from the truth. Honour where honour is due, and it does not in any way detract from her achievement to say that many men and women in all walks of life, and of every class of society, both in Belgium and northern France, cheerfully took risks, in helping men like Beaumont to escape, just as great as she did. His narrative confirms this statement to the full.

To some extent circumstances forced this on them. Some simply had to act as these men and women did. For in the retreat officers and men often got cut off from their units and left behind. Many of these, aided by civilians, managed to escape by way of the coast, and Beaumont, who paid frequent visits to Belgium after the war, to see the Belgians who had befriended him, and in so doing met many others who had helped British fugitives to get away, tells me how, in the confused period between the German invasion and their organisation of the territory they had overrun, many did get away on barges down the canals to the coast, often concealed in packing cases and barrels!

1. Their resistance was passive only, and directed solely against the regulations promulgated against hiding fugitive soldiers and helping men of military age to get away in order to join the armed forces of the Allies. They did not, with the exception of a few, deliberately transmit military information and none in this group attempted to interfere with the German military machine.

The man mainly responsible for this was Herman Capiau of Wasmes, an engineer working in the mining district round Mons, the Borinage or Belgian black country. He was an educated man and, a good linguist, had the advantage of being able to speak English and German fluently. According to Beaumont, Capiau got his first man away before the end of August. This was Major Gibbs of the Royal Field Artillery. Captain Taylor and Private Clark of the West Riding Regiment escaped by the same route later (see p. 54). It was also through Capiau and his friend Libiez, a lawyer and journalist in Mons, that Miss Cavell first came to start hiding soldiers in her nursing school. They brought Colonel Bodger and Sergeant Meachin of the Cheshire Regiment to her, and these two eventually travelled down the canals to Ghent. The former got caught. The latter managed to escape into Holland.

When Antwerp fell, and the Belgian Army retreated along the coast to link up with the British, the fighting line extended unbroken from the North Sea to the Swiss frontier, and there was now no obvious way of escape open to fugitives cut off behind it. Many, even some of the wounded, however, managed to evade capture for the time being. Some were hidden, and those wounded nursed, by peasants, small towns-people, miners, priests and nuns. Others threw away their uniforms and disguised themselves as labourers, miners or artisans. In consequence they now ran the risk of being shot as spies if they got caught.

Soon the position of these fugitives began to deteriorate. They had no money. Food started to run short. Further, the Germans, having consolidated the country they had occu-pied, posted notices to the effect that any Allied soldiers at large who did not give themselves up immediately would be shot, and any civilians, too, Belgian or French, who con-tinued to befriend them. In spite of this many, out of ordinary humanity, or out of patriotism and their hatred of the Germans, continued to befriend these men. Something had to be done, however, to save the situation. These guests had become a source of embarassment to their hosts and, unless they were to fall into the hands of the Germans in the end, some method had to be devised to get them out of the country. Soon it became apparent that the only way of doing this was to smuggle them across the Dutch frontier into neutral Holland.

In the Borinage, where Beaumont started his adventures, the initiative in this was again taken by Herman Capiau—he figures prominently in Beaumont's narrative—and his friend Albert Libiez. Together, as Libiez himself relates in a book published soon after the war,[1] they gradually collected the fugitives in the district and, having photographed them, disguised them, and provided them with faked passes—the château in Wasmes becoming the centre for this—they guided them, at great risk to themselves, into Brussels *en route* for the Dutch frontier. There they handed over some of them, at least, to Miss Cavell. She seems to have been known to Libiez through his father-in-law, Dr von Hassel, in whose makeshift aid post for the wounded he had been working.

South of the France-Belgian border the same sort of thing had been happening. Fugitives in hiding in the forest of Mormal were collected and guided under cover of darkness, again at great risk to themselves, by two young French women, Mlle Thuliez and Mlle Moriamé, to the Château of Bellignies, the home of Prince Réginald de Croy and his unmarried sister, the Princess Marie, both of Belgian nationality. Here these men were concealed while they were photographed by the Princess, and provided with forged identity cards the forms for which were scrounged during the

1. *L'affaire Cavell*, Albert Libiez, 1922.

lunch hour by the Belgian clerk working in the German office in Mons and stamped with a rubber stamp contrived by Derveau, the pharmacist in Mons, bearing the name of an imaginary commune. Then, like the fugitives from the Borinage, they were guided into Brussels by Mlle Thuliez, the Countess Jeanne de Belleville, a near neighbour, the Prince himself, and faithful members of his household.[1,2]

The de Croys and their helpers were playing the same part in organising the escape of fugitive soldiers into Holland from northern France as Capiau and Libiez were playing in the Belgian Borinage. Inevitably, particularly as all fugitives had to pass through Brussels, and the road and trams to Brussels ran through Mons, the two organisations, if such they can be called, loose associations of individuals bent on a common purpose, soon merged into one with its prominent and particularly active members, but no one actual leader. Before long, indeed, a definite system of passing fugitives through to Brussels had become established by mutual arrangement. From the Mormal district they were brought into the château at Bellignies; from the Borinage into the château at Wasmes. And, Wasmes being not far off the road from Bellignies to Mons, fugitives from northern France were also brought to Wasmes. Sometimes Capiau would meet parties from Bellignies at the frontier and guide them into Wasmes. He was peculiarly well placed for work of this kind. For, as mining engineer in the district, he had a permit which allowed him to travel round at all hours of the day or night, and it was easy for him to pass off any men with him as his workmen. This ruse never failed. For short local journeys women and children proved the best guides. They were less fearful than the men, and much less likely to excite suspicion. For the next and longer lap, Wasmes into

1. Princess Marie de Croy, *War Memories* (Macmillan & Co.), 1932.
2. Louise Thuliez, *Condemned to Death* (Methuen & Co.), 1934.

Brussels, or Bellignies to Brussels direct, adult guides needed to be found.

In Brussels itself, soon the centre of the German administration of occupied Belgium, these fugitives had, of course, to be kept hidden until such a time as guides and opportunity could be found to get them safely across the frontier into Holland, which, during the First World War, was not occupied by the Germans and remained neutral throughout. Many were lodged in Miss Cavell's hospital and school for nurses, but they were hidden by other patriots too, whose names have not gone down to history, among them Ada Bodart, the Irish widow of a Belgian, Louis Séverin, a chemist, Philippe Rasquin, the proprietor of a café, and a certain Mlle Marten, about whom I have been unable to discover anything. All this cost money, of course. Some of it was advanced by Miss Cavell out of school funds, and much probably put up by Georges Hostelet, secretary to M. Solway the banker, by Louis Séverin, and the de Croys. The rest of the cost was met by householders themselves.

Although, therefore, Miss Cavell played an important part in the work of the organisation, and her clinic and training school for nurses in the Rue de la Culture on the outskirts of German-occupied Brussels became the chief place where fugitives were hidden in the City, by no stretch of imagination can she be regarded as the originator of it. Rather, she was rushed into hiding soldiers in the first instance. Two fugitives in danger of their lives were brought to her by Capiau. Would she hide them? What Englishman, let alone a woman and a nurse, could possibly have refused? That is how she started. Once started on this dangerous course however, nothing would deter her. Her staff implored her to stop, but she would not, and this work soon began to take precedence over everything else. Nor did she merely hide fugitives and let others do the rest. All the evidence suggests that, when her house was full, she would find other accommodation for them somewhere, and that she played an active part in providing them with money and finding guides to take them to the frontier. We can never know all the facts now—nothing for obvious reasons was ever put down on paper—but she clearly collaborated closely with Baucq, the de Croys and Capiau, as I have endeavoured to describe in my book on her. She knew the risks. She must have realised that sooner or later she would be caught and punished, although I do not think she thought she would get shot. But it was her duty to serve her country in this way. And she gloried in it!

The third and last lap, Brussels to the frontier, and across it into Holland, was, of course, by far the most hazardous, and finding guides and planning routes to and across it was, as can be imagined, much the most difficult part of the total operation. Here Philippe Baucq, an architect who lived in Brussels, played the leading part. Guides of a kind were never difficult to get. Unemployment was rife, due to the British blockade of the coast, and guiding across the frontier quickly became a lucrative occupation. Poachers took to it readily, and smugglers who had previously smuggled goods now smuggled men. The difficulty was to find reliable ones, guides who would not lose their nerve and bolt at the critical moment, guides who would not, after a while, sell their secret to the Germans at a higher price. Miss Cavell employed two, both by the name of Gille, and Philippe Baucq, it is known, often planned the routes and guided parties of fugitives to the frontier himself.

The greatest difficulty that the organisation had to face was knowing whom to trust, and the reader should try to picture himself a civilian in enemy-occupied Belgium. This is peculiarly difficult for us to do, for, with the exception of the Channel Islands in the last war, this country has not been occupied since the Norman Conquest! Further, it must be remembered that, although the Germans had violated the neutrality of Belgium, their government was fully entitled, under International Law as it stood then, to promulgate and did promulgate all regulations necessary to ensure the security of their armed forces with very little regard for civilian rights. What was a Belgian to do? A man with no family responsibility could, of course, go 'underground', and serve the escape movement whole-heartedly. If he had no feeling for his country he could fraternise with the enemy, and then, if they won, he would finish his war in the best possible position for the future. Most found themselves in an intermediate position. They had family responsibility *and* patriotism, and often found themselves in terribly difficult positions in consequence. A man might have to work for the Germans, however much he hated it, in order to support his family. He also had to obey their regulations in order to keep himself out of prison. But what if a fugitive Allied soldier then turned up on his doorstep? What a conflict of loyalties! To what extent should he risk his own life, and the happiness and freedom of his family, to do his duty to his country? What a conflict of moral problems! Miss Cavell, for example, had been allowed by the Germans to continue her occupation as a nurse. So was she really justified in using the cover of nursing in order to further the Allied cause by helping British fugitives to escape and young Belgians to get away to join the armed forces of the Allies? She was not an army nurse. So she was not tied by the Geneva Convention, and although there is, and can be, no absolute answer to this question, few doubt that, under the circumstances in which she was placed, what she did was right. On the other hand, however unwise politically the Germans may have been, however harsh on European standards their military law at the time, under International

Law, as it stood then, they were legally, in spite of the fact that they had violated the neutrality of Belgium, justified in the execution of Miss Cavell. She was helping the Allied cause. Germany now had to fight the war, and this kind of thing had to be stopped. 'It may sometimes be the duty of an individual to do something,' writes Hastings Rashdall, 'which, nevertheless, it may be the right and duty of other individuals to shoot him for doing.' And this was written in quite a different context![1]

Considerations of this kind must be borne in mind in reading this remarkable book. It is a fascinating individual story against the set-up of the escape organisation as a whole which I have now endeavoured to describe in brief, portraying at the same time the ups and downs of bourgeois Belgian life under German occupation. Mine, indeed, was a stroke of luck to have found it, and it is now a privilege to introduce its author, an 'old contemptible', and the many Belgians who risked their lives to help him, to the British and, I very much hope, also to the Belgian public.

1. P. E. Matheson, *The Life of Hastings Rashdall, D.D.* (Oxford University Press), 1928.

I

Blind collision

In the early morning of the 20th August 1914 the 1st Battalion of the Queen's Own Royal West Kent Regiment, a unit of the 13th Infantry Brigade, British Expeditionary Force, moved out of the French town of Landrecies *en route* for Mons in Belgium, of which, at that time, few people had even heard. It was, we were told, forty miles away!

Many of us had been drawn, like myself, from the Army Reserve which had been called up at the outbreak of war, men who sixteen days before had been engaged in their various callings in civilian life. So, although we were all trained soldiers, we were not really at that time fit to undertake the forced march required of us under the conditions then prevailing. Those of us who had come directly from sedentary occupations were much out of physical condition.

We were saddled with pack and equipment weighing nearly eighty pounds, and our khaki uniforms, flannel shirts, and thick woollen pants, fit for an Arctic climate, added to our discomfort in the sweltering heat. By midday the temperature reached ninety degrees in the shade! We were soon soaked with perspiration, and all looked almost as if they had been dragged through water!

Some of the regulations, no doubt framed for our benefit, seemed petty, and were correspondingly resented. Smoking cigarettes on the march, for example, was forbidden, although addicts to a pipe were allowed to puff away to their hearts' content. This rule was unfair, and died a natural death on the first day. It was afterwards officially rescinded. Another one was 'no drinking from water-bottles without orders'. This was, no doubt, a necessary regulation, and was strictly enforced. The pitiless rays of the sun, and the dust rising from the road, fostered an intolerable thirst however, and soon some way simply had to be found to extract water from one's bottle without being detected. So when one bright spark plucked a straw from the corn growing by the wayside, inserted it into his bottle, and sucked his water up through it, the idea spread through the ranks. Not a man was discovered disobeying orders in this way, but our officers must have wondered why so many of their men had suddenly taken a liking to sucking straws!

The end of the first day's march found us at Les Maroilles. There we billeted for the night and, as soon as we were settled in, we quickly discarded our wet shirts and hung them up to dry, putting on our worsted cardigan jackets instead. These we soon found were terribly irritating and uncomfortable garments to wear next to one's skin. It was them or nothing however. All spare clothing had been withdrawn at the Base for the use of those coming on behind. How unprepared Britain was for war! She could not even provide her 1st Army with a spare shirt!

The following morning, August 21st, we woke stiff and sore to find that the weather showed every sign of being as hot as on the previous day, and before moving off many of us cast our thick woollen pants. These we left in our billets. Many French peasants that day came into possession of garments which they no doubt regarded as gifts from the gods. Anyway, they could keep them. We at least were a little cooler without them.

At midday we left France behind, and crossed the border into Belgium. Here the local population gave us a great welcome, and showed their appreciation of our arrival by showering gifts of fruit, food and cigarettes on us. Soon after this, too, the brigade left the road, and entered a meadow for the midday halt, and had scarcely settled down before, from a little village nestling among the trees about two hundred yards up the road, a crowd of peasants approached, carrying milk churns and huge baskets of bread. One of their number then asked our brigadier for permission to present food and coffee to his troops. This was quickly granted, and we were paraded for the distribution to take place.

It was a sight to see those peasant women slicing up large loaves, while their men plastered on the butter, and their children walked down the ranks making the distribution. It was a mystery how a small village of not more than forty cottages could manage to feed three thousand men in this way—and three thousand hungry men at that!

After this we resumed our march, and within an hour began to feel the effects of the intense heat. Some were soon more or less in a state of collapse, and had to be supported by their comrades, while others carried their rifles. We struggled on however, and late that afternoon, with perspiration streaming down our faces, causing our sun-burned skin to smart, just as if it had been scratched and then rubbed with salt, we arrived at the town of Bavay.

Next morning, August 22nd, we paraded for the third day's march, which would, we were told, bring us in the vicinity of Mons. Before moving off we charged magazines. It was understood that we were likely to meet the enemy during the day. Further, as it had been impossible to get our shirts dry during the night, many of us tried wearing our cardigan jackets under our tunics, spreading our wet shirts across our packs to dry in the sun as we marched. These so irritated our skin, however, that at the midday halt we were all glad to revert to our damp, filthy, and now smelly shirts.

The temperature still continued round about ninety degrees in the shade, and in the afternoon a few men collapsed and had to be brought along behind by ambulance. In spite of it all, at about 6 p.m., a weary battalion limped painfully into the village of Hornu, five miles north-west of Mons. New boots on rough roads and cobbled streets had blistered our feet to such an extent that when we halted some of us could hardly stand!

That night 'B' Company, to which I belonged, secured billets in a farm. The farmer and his hands were busily engaged in threshing the corn recently gathered in from the fields, and, except for differences in language and dress, one could have imagined oneself back in our own English countryside. It was like home to many of our men whose work had been on the land.

After a wash in the duck pond, a tidy-up, and something to eat, a comrade and I got on top of a manure heap so as to get a view of what was going on in the street. This ran parallel to the wall on one side of our yard, and across the way stood a little estaminet where an old gramophone was laboriously grinding out well-worn records. Every now and then the needle would stick on a circle, and repeat the same phrase over and over again, until the owner helped it into the next groove. People passed and looked up at us in curiosity. Some tried to talk to us in French, and before long a young priest came along, started to do so in passable English, and must have noticed that we were casting longing eyes towards the estaminet. For he soon invited us to have a drink and, being old soldiers and afraid of breaking tradition, we naturally consented, and he returned a few moments later with a girl carrying a tray and two large mugs of beer. Our comrades down below looked up at us with envious eyes. Soon after this he wished us good luck, and departed on his way.

We were now just thinking of turning in when we heard the drone of an aeroplane coming from the east. All eyes were turned that way. Was it a German one? And in those days all aircraft were still something of a novelty. When it came in sight everyone was impressed by its beauty. But it was a German. At a great height, and against a perfect summer sky too, its outline resembled a gigantic hawk searching for its prey, and after circling round the district it disappeared in the direction from which it came.

That night orders were received that the battalion would remain at Hornu the next day (Sunday), and proceed to Mons on the Monday. This was good news. A rest was sorely needed to clean up and pull ourselves together, and on that Sunday (August 23rd) we emerged from our beds of hay in the barn on a perfect, quiet, and peaceful summer morning. After breakfast there were the usual 'spit and polish' parades according to the routine of an army in the field followed by an inspection by the Brigadier, who complimented us on the way we had stuck the march. Indeed, he seemed very pleased until he spotted that a number of us had 'lost' our cap badges and regimental numerals, bartered, of course, for a packet of cigarettes or swopped for a kiss from some pretty French girl on the march up. But too many of us had done it for anyone actually to get punished.

The company now broke up into small groups, discussing the job we had in hand and our chances of success. All agreed that the war would be over before Christmas. In the short time, too, that we had been on active service a spirit of comradeship between us all, among officers, N.C.O.s and men, seemed to have been born such as had never really existed before. We had faith in our leaders, and confidence in our ability to win through any task that we might be called upon to perform. In the days that followed, this confidence, it is true, was to be rudely shattered, and at times almost dissipated, but in spite of all our adversities that spirit of comradeship survived to the end of the war. Today it still exists among those of us who are left, and knows no caste, creed or politics. No greater brotherhood has ever existed in the whole history of man.

On that Sunday morning we had another opportunity to study village life. Some of the inhabitants brought their children to see the British troops who had come to their rescue. Others were to be seen on their way to mass in response to the bell calling them to morning prayer. Yet, in these surroundings of peace and happiness, death and destruction followed in the brief space of an hour.

The cattle were still grazing quietly on the scorched pastures, and the worshippers were now returning from mass, gaily chatting to one another as they walked up the long white dusty road stretching like a ribbon into the distance, when all of a sudden the tranquillity of the scene was broken by the short sharp bark of field guns, followed by shells screaming overhead and bursting in all directions. The villagers rushed to their homes in panic, slammed their doors, fastened their shutters, and were seen no more. We seized our equipment, fell in, and quickly started off at the double to take up the position which, as a precautionary measure, had been allotted to us overnight. As we entered a belt of tall fir trees, shrapnel burst overhead, cutting off branches as clean as if they had been severed by a woodman's axe. Some optimist said they were our own shells falling short! In any event they were far too close to be comfortable, and for many of us it was our baptism of fire. Nevertheless, except that they made us increase our pace, everyone appeared outwardly calm.

On reaching the open country the company split up into platoons, each under its own commander. Mine then moved to the right of a slag-heap, situated to our immediate front,

our orders being to advance along a canal until we reached
St Ghislain. On reaching the canal we moved round in front
of the slag-heap. Here we got our first sight of the enemy,
advancing in mass formation with their front rank firing from
the hip. It was like watching a military tattoo at Aldershot!
But their aim was high, and their bullets only buried themselves in the top of the slag-heap towering a hundred feet
above and behind us. We had not advanced far, however,
before we found that the ground between the slag-heap and
the canal was so waterlogged as to be impassable, and we
were compelled to return to our original starting point, and
set out again by a different route. Half an hour later we
made contact with the remainder of the company, and
entered the village of St Ghislain. This already showed signs
of damage by enemy gunfire. The streets were strewn with
bricks and masonry, and a gaping hole half-way down the
steeple showed that the church had received attention from
the German gunners.

We had now been in contact with the enemy for the best
part of an hour, and the effects of the strain of the three days'
march from Landrecies to Hornu were becoming apparent.
Packs seemed to weigh hundredweights, instead of pounds.
So, when one man had the courage to chance the consequences, and discarded his pack, we all followed his example
and felt as if we had been relieved of millstones that had long
been hanging round our necks. We were tired and weary and
hungry men, indeed, who went into action that afternoon,
but, as we passed down the village street, cottage doors
opened just sufficiently for the occupants to pass out gifts of
food, wine and cigarettes. In most cases only the arm of the
donor was to be seen. These we grabbed thankfully as we
ran, gifts which seemed to have been sent by Providence in
lieu of our dinners. The latter had disappeared with the
cookers at the first sound of coming battle.

C

In skeleton order we advanced over the bridge at St Ghislain, and took up a position in a glass factory on the opposite side of the canal. Its walls were quickly loopholed. Here, concealed from the enemy's view, and covered from his shell-fire, we came into action for the first time.

The country in front of our position was flat, and dotted with numerous circular fenced-in copses, a common feature in that part of Belgium. The Germans, moving between them, made easy targets, and we opened fire. Their losses that afternoon must have been tremendous. Further, our two battalion machine guns created havoc among the enemy when they attempted to outflank our position by crossing the railway, which ran at right angles and to the right of it, skirted on each side by wooded slopes, straight ahead as far as the eye could see. For, hidden between abandoned locomotives at a point where it was crossed by another line, running on an embankment parallel with the canal at our rear, they commanded it and before nightfall many bodies in field grey could be seen strewn in the permanent way.

As darkness fell we vacated the factory for a new position, on the embankment at our rear, where we remained silent, waiting; and, within an hour, heard sounds that left no doubt in our minds that the Germans were moving up their guns and transport. But silence was still the watchword, and by 10 p.m. they had advanced so close that we could hear them talking! Hearing no sound from us they had naturally come to the conclusion that we had withdrawn, and small fires began to spring up all over the place, presumably for cooking their evening meals. This was asking for trouble on their part, and just to show them that we were still here, and taking those fires as our targets, we opened out with fifteen rounds 'rapid fire', known in the Army as the 'mad minute', that 'mad minute' which led the German

High Command to think, during those early days of the war, that the British infantry were heavily armed with machine guns! Judging from the cries of the wounded and the general commotion that followed, our fire must have found many targets in the dark. In any case we had given them a surprise. Their fires died out as quickly as they had appeared and, with the exception of a restive horse champing its bit, silence reigned again.

About midnight we received orders to retire across the canal, and at 1 a.m. on August 24th we were told that a general retirement was about to begin. In view of the previous day's fighting, and the heavy losses we had inflicted on the Germans, this news was received with consternation. It was almost unbelievable! But a few moments later the shrill note of a whistle was followed by a deafening roar as the St Ghislain bridge went up into the air. The Retreat from Mons had begun![1]

After a short delay we started to move off in the darkness. Nobody seemed to know our destination. It was just a matter of following the party in front, and we had not got far before we found the road blocked with guns, limbers, wagons and all the paraphernalia of war. Their progress seemed terribly slow, and so was ours, but, apart from their rumbling and the

1. Captain Walter Bloem, of the Brandenburg Grenadiers, in his *Advance from Mons, 1914*, translated by G. C. Wynne and published by Peter Davies Ltd, 1930, gives a detailed account of his experiences as a Company Commander in the attack on the position held by the West Kents and other units of the 13th Infantry Brigade on the canal bank near St Ghislain, and describes the shock the Germans got when they first encountered, entirely contrary to what they had been led to expect, highly trained troops, after their easy 'walk' through east Belgium, and the devastating fire of the British. He admits that they would have been annihilated, had they been counter-attacked; and describes their amazement and relief when the British withdrew across the canal, blowing up the bridge over it at 1.30 a.m. the following morning. His story confirms Beaumont's statements, and as an account of the battle, from the other side, affords fascinating reading.   *Editor*

occasional bark of a dog, not a sound was now to be heard. All of us were both too tired and too disappointed to talk.

Two hours later we succeeded in getting clear of the traffic by passing into a narrow lane which branched off the main road, and, two miles further on, became aware that we were followed by a solitary horseman. Our subaltern, being curious, instructed the last two sections of our platoon to remain with him to see who he was and, as he loomed up out of the darkness, no one was more surprised than we were ourselves to see that he was a Uhlan. Finding that he was heavily outnumbered, he offered no resistance and dismounted. He was our first prisoner. Our officer, being able to speak German, now asked him many questions. He said that he had been an advance scout. Early the previous afternoon he had been cut off by the English, who he did not realise were in the vicinity, before he could get back to the canal, and, finding himself cut off, had hidden in a wood until nightfall. Later, hearing troops on the move, he had followed them, thinking they were his own! He did not seem the least perturbed at having been taken prisoner but, in case he tried to escape, one man was sent ahead with his horse, while the rest, acting as his escort, hurried him along to join the battalion.

Later, as the grey streaks of dawn were being heralded by the red flashes from a battery of British guns perched on a slag-heap on our left flank, we dropped down a hill into the mining village of Wasmes, six miles west of Mons, where, little though I knew it then, I was destined to spend the next seven months of my life; seven months of adventure, hopes and disappointments in which I shared the home life, and the joys and sorrows, of its inhabitants, an experience which befell few men during the Great War.

The roll was called in the village square, and we found that after half a day's fighting our casualties amounted to one man killed and two missing. We then fell out to await the arrival of the cookers. These, as usual, were conspicuous by their absence. Some of my companions now simply slumped to the ground, where they stood, and were soon fast asleep. Others, of whom I was one, wandered about the square to see if there was anything to be scrounged. And we were lucky in our search! We discovered a brewery. There two Belgians were handing out beer free of charge to all and sundry, before the Germans arrived. How this little affair might have ended there is no knowing, but we began to get a little hilarious, and some actually burst into song. These were unexpected sounds to emanate from exhausted troops, and quickly attracted a staff officer to the spot. He broke up the party.

We were not allowed much of a rest. At 8.30 the Germans started to shell the village, causing a few casualties among civilians and troops before they could take cover, and half an hour later my company received orders to advance out of it to a position near the spot where we had seen the British battery in action at dawn. A company of the Duke of Wellington's Regiment were hard-pressed at that point. We should find, we were told, trenches there, which had been prepared by the Royal Engineers during the brief time we had been resting, and that our job now was to delay the enemy, while the rest of the battalion carried on with the retirement. In other words we were to fight a rearguard action and, if necessary, sacrifice ourselves in order to allow others to escape.

The village of Wasmes lies in a depression, and in order to reach our objective we had to climb a steep hill on the left of which was a high wall in a state of crumbling decay. Behind this was a bank sloping upwards, forming a high ridge covered with young trees. All those at the top had been cut down recently, however, leaving about six inches of stump protruding from the ground. On the right of the hill was open country. Here and there the roadway was strewn with broken and twisted telegraph wires. These had been cut by the German gun-fire half an hour previously.

On nearing the top of the hill the company passed through a gap in the wall, and took cover in the wood that ran along the ridge, but my platoon, emerging from the wood, which terminated with the ridge at the top of the hill, found themselves on the edge of a cornfield. The corn had been cut, and stood in stooks ready for carrying, and about a hundred and fifty yards distant we could see the position which we were about to occupy. We extended to 'open order' at six paces distance, with four officers behind the line, and in blissful ignorance advanced across the stubble.

We had not covered more than thirty yards when the Germans rose from those very trenches we were intending to occupy, and met us with withering fire at close range which wiped out most of that gallant platoon before anyone realised what had happened. The few that escaped their first volley rushed forward and tried to return the enemy's fire from behind the stooks. Others fired from a kneeling position from the line where they stood.

My position was at the extreme right of our line, and immediately following the enemy's first burst of fire I felt a sharp stab in my groin. I knew that I was hit and, seeing that we were hopelessly outnumbered, dropped to the ground, with both arms outstretched and my head turned to one side. The least movement on my part would have brought certain death from those trenches such a short distance away, and, to make matters worse, the Germans now brought a machine gun into action. This pumped streams of lead into those stooks of corn, and from where I lay I saw each of my unfortunate comrades, who had taken cover behind them, wiped out in turn. This accomplished, the gunner turned his attention to the line, or rather to what was left of it. Three times he traversed it, and three times I waited for death. But although I was smothered with earth and stubble, ploughed up by his bullets as they struck the ground all round me, that never came. I was never hit again![1]

Behind me stood a huge heap of manure and if only I could get behind that, I felt that I would be safe, for the moment at least. Gradually the enemy's fire died down. Then it ceased altogether. This was my opportunity. Scrambling to my feet, and leaving my rifle behind, I made one bold dash for that heap, which I reached without another shot being fired at me! I found three other survivors there, all wounded. In those few ghastly minutes we must have lost four officers and forty-five men killed outright. For the element of surprise is all important in battle, and viewing the events of the night before, and assuming that all bridges over the canal had been destroyed, I cannot now help giving the Germans full credit for the rapidity with which they re-bridged the canal, enabling them to follow so closely on our heels.

Leaving the friendly manure-heap we four survivors of my unlucky platoon now limped back into the wood. There we met a corporal, who told us that the remainder of the company had retired, and that we were to follow on. But the enemy artillery had again become active, and now com-

1. There is no mention of this disastrous episode in which Beaumont was wounded in G. T. Atkinson's *Queen's Own Royal West Kent Regiment, 1914–1918*, published by Simpkin, Marshall, Hamilton, Kent & Co. 1914. There were too few survivors, perhaps, to tell the tale. But it confirms the rest of Beaumont's story, and relates how A and B Companies were sent to help the Duke of Wellington's hard-pressed Battalion and how Beaumont's own Company Commander, Major Pack Beresford, was killed leading his men forward. Nor does the official history of the Regiment give any account of Beaumont's subsequent adventures.
Editor

menced shelling the wood as we were passing through. So, thinking it safer to have a wall between me and the direction from which these shells were coming, I slipped down the bank behind it. I had not gone far, however, before there was a blinding flash, followed by a deafening roar, as a shell hit the base of the wall at the very spot I was passing at that moment. I saw the wall split and topple towards me, and made one frantic effort to get clear by throwing myself backwards up the bank. In so doing, however, the heel of my right boot got wedged between stumps of trees, and with all the breath knocked out of my body I was pinned to the bank from the waist downwards by several hundredweight of brickwork with the upper part of my body embedded in the undergrowth.

Seeking safety I had met disaster. Still I felt thankful to be alive, and struggled frantically to drag myself free. Those tree-stumps held my foot as in a vice. I tried to move the brickwork. This proved beyond my strength, and I was reluctant to call for help. This could only have brought the Germans to the spot, and something—it may have been instinct—told me not to do that. In the circumstances I could do nothing, and resigned myself to wait for whatever might turn up, but at length, with a desperate effort, managed to wriggle free of my equipment. Then, with my cap over my face, I must have fallen off to sleep from sheer exhaustion.

Editor's postscript. From the *Official History of the War. Military Operations France and Belgium, 1914,* p. 71.

'Having cleared the advance party of the West Kents, who had gone forward beyond the canal (A. Company), out of their way, the *Brandenburg Grenadiers* swarmed forward over the maze of barbed wire fences against their main position on the canal. This, however, was so well concealed that the German artillery failed to discover it, and the progress of the German infantry was slow and costly, the attack on the bridge at St Ghislain being halted 300 yards from the canal by the accurate fire of the West Kents. The Germans imagined that they were opposed everywhere by machine guns only, not realising the intensity of British rifle fire. Walter Bloem of the *Brandenburg Grenadiers* lost all his Company officers and half his men. That evening, too, his commanding officer said to him: "You are my sole support. My only Company Commander left. The Battalion is a wreck—my proud, beautiful battalion." Bloem himself adds: "Our first battle was a heavy unheard of defeat—and against the English, the English we laughed at!" '

2

Befriended

W HEN I awoke another day had dawned, and from the position of the sun I judged it to be about ten o'clock. I had had a long sleep, but did not feel refreshed. My wound was painful and both my legs felt dead. Indeed, I had the uncomfortable feeling that I was dying from below upwards! I was also hungry and parched with thirst, but my haversack was empty and my water-bottle crushed and no longer capable of holding water, and in spite of the pitiless rays of the August sun I felt chilled to the bone. Further, except for a few noisy sparrows quarrelling in the trees behind, I was alone and with only my thoughts for company. These were mixed, and anything but pleasant.

By supporting myself on my elbows I found that I was just able to see over the top of the mass of brickwork which was pinning me down, and also that I had an unbroken view over open country for about a thousand yards until another wood blocked my further view. So I scanned the intervening space and, before long, saw a party of Germans busily engaged in searching the bodies of both British and Germans who had fallen the day before, the khaki and field-grey uniforms of the dead showing up plainly in the bright sunlight. Again I wanted to call for help. But again instinct, or whatever else you like to call it, prompted me not to do that. In any case they were too far away for me to have been able to make them hear had I attempted to call out.

An hour later I heard the sound of footsteps approaching up the hill, and, as the sounds came nearer, I cautiously peered over the brickwork. Two civilians now appeared in line with the gap in the wall. Assuming that they were Belgians, and presumably friends, I shouted to attract their attention. And friends they proved to be! In a very few moments they had freed me from my uncomfortable prison, although it took their combined strength, using a piece of timber as a lever, to lift the brickwork off my legs. Again I had had a lucky escape. I could see now that other tree-stumps had kept it suspended six inches or more off the bank. The same agent that had held me prisoner had saved both my legs from being crushed!

These two Belgians now carried me up the bank to the wood at the top, where they set me on my feet but, having lost the use of both legs, I was unable to stand and was obliged to clutch at them for support. So I sat down, took off my puttees and commenced massaging my legs. The Belgians, seeing what I was trying to do, took the job out of my hands, and with one working on each leg my circulation in them was gradually restored. At this moment we heard the sound of marching troops in the distance. One of the Belgians immediately darted to the edge of the wood, and coming back, spoke one word to his companion—'*Allemands!*' Whereupon they bolted out on the opposite side as fast as their legs could carry them.

It was obvious that those troops coming down the road by the wall could only be Germans. So I crawled into the undergrowth, and remained there till the sound of their heavy tramping had died away in the distance, and, expecting the Belgians to return, remained waiting there some time. As the day wore on, however, and they did not come back, I decided to move, now being very hungry and in pain, and left the wood in the same direction as the Belgians. In my dazed condition I found walking difficult, but managed to stagger along over ploughed fields and pasture land until I came to the outskirts of a village.

All the way from the wood to the village I did not see a soul, either Belgian or German, and I now proceeded to reconnoitre it. Soon I came upon the dried-up bed of a stream, along which I now crawled until it entered a tunnel about three feet six inches in diameter. This ran under the Place du Wasmes, situated in the centre of the village, and it appealed to me as an ideal hiding-place. So I crept in, and found it very good for observation of the cottages in view on either side of the dried-up stream. I could see without being seen, and watched patiently for some sign of life that might be the means of getting something to eat, but, by the time darkness fell, I had not seen a soul enter or leave any of those cottages. Indeed, for all the signs of life there were the village might have been stricken by a plague which had wiped out its entire population, and I was afraid to go and beg food, hungry though I was, from any of those cottages. They might be occupied by Germans.

With bitter thoughts about war, and everything connected with it, I fell asleep, to be woken up very soon by the rumble of heavy wagons and the tramp of marching feet, as German transport and troops passed across the Place du Wasmes immediately above my head. How I cursed those Germans for disturbing my night's rest! Considering the time those noises continued they must have been moving up heavy reinforcements that night. Then silence fell again, and I was able to go to sleep once more. I do not know how long I slept, but I woke with a start. Something soft and furry had touched my hand and, as I scrambled into a sitting position, I heard an army of rats scamper away over the loose pebbles that lay on the floor of my tunnel. I don't suppose there were really very many of them, and I could not see them, but the experience was uncanny and in my imagination they numbered hundreds! So, as I was not anxious to offer myself as a meal for rats, I left my hiding-place, and finished the night undisturbed in some long grass outside.

In the morning I was woken by the tinkle of a bicycle bell and, peering through the grass, I saw a German cyclist, not more than six yards away, although he never saw me! As soon as he had gone on his way, I lost no time in getting back to my tunnel. A little later I heard great activity overhead, and in spite of the danger curiosity was now strong enough to bring me out of my tunnel again to see what it was all about, and I was just able, by climbing on to a low bridge, to see across the Place du Wasmes. There, through a slit in the boarding on top of the parapet, I saw a battery of German artillery harnessing up their horses. That sent me scuttling back again.

By midday the pangs of hunger compelled me to leave my hiding-place, and take the risk of being caught. So I crawled up the bed of the stream until I came level with a cottage which stood back from all the others and was well out of sight of the Place du Wasmes. With my heart in my mouth I scrambled up the bank and knocked at the door. This, after some delay, was opened by an old woman who, when she saw a dirty, scruffy British soldier, with three days' growth of stubble on his chin, standing there in front of her, threw up her hands in horror. But, before she had had time to recover, I was pleading: '*Du pain, café—du pain, café.*' She did not invite me to step in, for which I did not blame her, but she nodded instead, and signed to me that I was to stay where I was by pointing to the ground where I stood. I waited, and in a few moments she returned and handed me a chunk of bread and a bowl of coffee. These I wolfed like a ravenous dog. Never in all my life had I imagined that dry bread could taste so good. It proved to me that those who have never wanted cannot really know what it is like to have to go without.

I knocked at the door and returned the bowl to the old woman. As I could not speak her language, I could not thank her. So, to show my gratitude, I seized her rough and kindly hand and kissed it, a gesture which made tears roll down her weather-beaten face. Then I turned my back on the cottage and made my way towards the open country.

Food had put new life into me, but my senses were dazed, and I could not think. My only desire was to walk, and keep on walking, and in this mood, without any definite object or sense of direction, I wandered over hill and dale without seeing either man or beast until after about an hour I began to feel utterly weary. My groin also started to hurt horribly. So, seeing a house standing alone, I turned in that direction, and when within a short distance of it saw the door open and a young Belgian come out to meet me. I had reached the end of my tether, but with his help I staggered the rest of the way, and sat down on the doorstep while he had a good look round to make sure we had not been observed. Then he invited me in.

Three children were playing on the floor. They looked up and, when they saw my uniform, gave one terrified scream, ran to their mother, who was sitting by the fire, and buried their heads in her lap. Their terror was hardly to be wondered at. Two days before a battle had raged near, and perhaps around, that very house, and it was easy to imagine the effect that the rattle of musketry and machine guns and the scream of shells must have had on those three little children. They had probably had a visit from the Germans, too, as they passed through, which perhaps had proved anything but gentle so far as the woman was concerned. This alone could have made them afraid of any uniform, but they were soon pacified by their parents, although they regarded me with suspicion until their father came over and kissed me on both cheeks. This gesture of friendship put them at their ease, and before I left we had all become the best of pals.

The kind woman soon prepared a meal for me: hot coffee, bread, butter and raw eggs! This simple fare was to me, still a hungry man, a feast; and if ever I had longed to be able to speak French it was at that moment. I was more than grateful for what I had received, but I could only show my gratitude by nodding my head like an idiot. Action, however, sometimes speaks louder than words. I think they understood.

After this, and a brief rest, my new-found friend took me into another room, apparently their bedroom. Like their living-room this was also almost in darkness. All windows in the house were still shuttered and barred, as they had been while the fighting was going on outside, but sunbeams filtered through cracks like bands of gold. Then, having closed the door, he signed to me, by beginning to do it himself, that he wished me to take off all my clothes. Not understanding his motive, but entirely in his hands, I did as he wanted, and removed everything except my shirt. But he wanted that off as well! This puzzled me a little. Nevertheless, just to please him, off it came!

Seeing that I was wounded, he now ran out of the room, and returned with a bowl of warm water and some rags. The latter were neither white nor clean, but it led me to remember the first field dressing which every soldier carries in his tunic. So I extracted my own. This was the first opportunity I had had to look at the wound which I had got now some forty-eight hours previously. I knew that I had stopped something, and could now feel that this something was still there in my groin. But it did not feel large, or look deep enough to be serious. So, after my meal and dressing my wound, I began to feel a new man, and wanting a good wash,

I went through the motions of rubbing soap on my hands and washing my face and, pointing to the bowl of water, exclaimed '*Encore*', one of the very few French words I knew. He was puzzled at first, but at length understood me. Soon I was able to have almost a bath in nearly a gallon of water.

When I turned round the Belgian had disappeared. And so had all my clothes! Thinking that he had taken them away to clean, I now popped into the bed. I was naked, and afraid someone else might come in. There I waited wondering, and after a little while he returned, but, instead of giving me back my uniform, he handed me a civilian suit, complete with cap and pants and shirt! The only item of my own property which he brought back was my boots!

Not being able to speak his language, and the Belgian not being able to speak mine, I could not ask the reason for this sudden change into 'civvies', but, as I had to wear something, I lost no time in getting into them. Then I was taken back to the living-room, where my nostrils were instantly assailed by the smell of burning wool and, glancing towards the fire, I saw the last of my khaki uniform going up in smoke! I must confess that I was puzzled and annoyed, annoyed because I had lost my army papers and other things in the pockets of my uniform. The former could not be replaced. The latter were valuable for sentimental or other reasons, and to have these all destroyed by a stranger, without so much as asking by your leave, was enough to upset anyone. However, they were gone beyond recovery now, and it was no use protesting when my friend could not understand a word of English.

One fact stood out above all others. By burning my uniform and providing me with a civilian suit, he had placed me in a position which would be difficult to explain to either friend or foe. If by any chance I was able to regain the British lines, I should be open to be tried for desertion. If I

e author, shortly after the First World War   Arthur Heath

Mme Neusy

Emile Neusy

fell into the hands of the Germans, which was much more likely, I should no doubt be regarded as a spy. And the penalty for both offences was death! I was between the devil, on the one hand, and the deep blue sea on the other, and the Belgian, seeing that I was upset at the loss of my uniform, sat me in a chair and gently patted me on the back, like a father trying to soothe a troubled child. This action made me think that perhaps, after all, he had a good reason for the drastic thing that he had done.

After a few minutes' earnest conversation with his wife, the man left the house, and alone with her and the children I felt a little lost. I wanted something to occupy my mind, something to distract my thoughts from the awful events of the last forty-eight hours. At first I attempted to talk with the woman by signs. This was not a success. She did not seem to cotton on. So I turned my attention to the children. They seemed to understand me much better, and tried to entice me into a game which appeared to be the Belgian equivalent of 'Ring-a-Roses'. Then, as I did not feel capable of jumping about, they started other games in which I could at least take some part sitting down. Hearing their delighted cries now helped me to forget.

After about an hour the Belgian returned, and made signs for me to leave the house and follow him. So, bidding his wife goodbye, and kissing the children, who seemed to be rather sad at losing their new-found playmate, I left in his company and, on reaching the roadway, we started in the direction of a colliery surrounded by slag-heaps towering like miniature mountains above it. It was some distance and, as we approached a triangular patch of green which separated a fork in the road, I saw the bodies of fifteen to twenty British soldiers piled in a heap. They might have been so much garbage! Some were almost naked, and their bodies had been literally slashed to pieces, trails of blood on the

D

road showing that they had been dragged together through the dust. (I was unable to see to what regiments they had belonged for, like so many others, these had evidently bartered their cap badges and numerals on the way up to Mons.) Those men had obviously been the victims of frenzy, brutally done to death after they had been wounded, murdered by a foe who were drunk with victory, a foe who before the war had boasted of their culture and their Christianity.

Nearby on a grassy bank, too, lay a Belgian with both hands in his trouser pockets and his cap tilted over his face. At first I thought he was asleep in the sun. A closer look revealed that he was dead, shot through the head! No doubt he had been an accidental witness of this awful crime. And dead men tell no tales![1]

The horror of that scene will remain in my memory as long as I live. As I gazed at it that afternoon I was held spellbound, until my Belgian friend took me kindly by the arm, and led me gently on our way towards the colliery where, on arrival, I was piloted to a room which had evidently been in recent use as an operating theatre. There was blood everywhere, pools on the floor, on the sodden bed-linen, and even splashes of it on the white tiled walls. In fact the place had the appearance of a slaughter house, and while passing from this room to another, a Belgian came out carrying a man's leg, foot upwards, in a bucket. This was the last straw. This sickening sight, coupled with the events of the last forty-eight hours, was too much for me altogether. All

1. On the hill above Wasmes stands a memorial erected by the villagers to the men who died there. One side is dedicated to the Belgian civilians shot by the Germans, another to the French, and a third to the memory of members of the 13th and 14th Infantry Brigade of the B.E.F. who fell in the fighting round it. There are no names on the side dedicated to the British; instead a bronze plaque portrays a scene during the retreat.   *Author*

the horror and ghastliness of war loomed up in front of me like an awful nightmare, and I collapsed on the floor.

I was soon on the operating table under the examination of two doctors, and while one smothered me with a towel, the other extracted a piece of metal from my groin. This proved to be the nickel casing of a German bullet, and a young man standing by informed me in perfect English that I was lucky to be alive. If it had penetrated a fraction of an inch deeper, he said, it would have severed my femoral artery. Then I should have bled to death in a few minutes. Considering also all that had happened after I was hit, I too also thought I had been lucky.

I was then taken to a building on the other side of the road and given a clean shirt. I shall never forget that shirt. It was all front, complete with pleats, and 'did up' at the back—a typical Belgian product. Then I was taken to a room where there were about twenty other British soldiers, and, as soon as I was safely tucked up in bed, my Belgian friend, who had not left my side since we entered the colliery, kissed me on both cheeks and left the building. Only when, some days later, I wanted to get up, did I discover that he had taken my clothes away with him! Still, after all, they were his, and he had a perfect right to take them. But it did make things awkward. I did own my army boots, but my shirt was on loan, and these two articles constituted my entire wardrobe!

Lying in bed gave me time to think, and ask questions of the Belgians working in this colliery hospital, one of whom could speak good English, as to how the Germans had treated the inhabitants when they entered the village. On August 24th, I was told, sixteen miners had been shot for no other 'crime' than sitting on a wall to watch them as they advanced on the heels of the retiring British. They were ordered off it, and made to dig a trench, and before that was two feet deep were shot and buried in it. Six months later

I heard that the Belgian authorities obtained permission from the German commandant of the area to exhume their bodies for decent burial in the local cemetery.

This information cleared up much that had hitherto been a mystery to me. Terror reigned in the district, and its inhabitants were afraid to venture abroad when any Germans were about. It accounted for the absence of people in the village during my sojourn in the tunnel, and also for not seeing anybody when I was wandering at large. It also explained the reason for the destruction of my uniform and papers, and my journey to the hospital in a civilian suit. My Belgian friend knew more about Germans and their ways than I did at that time.

3

Colliery hospital

AFTER a week in bed, with the time divided between sleeping and listening to the dull booming of the heavy German guns bombarding Maubeuge, eight miles away, the wound in my groin began to heal and I soon asked the doctor for permission to get up. At the same time I explained that I had no clothes. I was told however that I would find plenty of uniforms in the store-room and that, as the owners would never require them again, I could take my choice. Naturally I did not altogether relish the idea of wearing dead men's khaki but, as the choice was Hobson's, I fitted myself out as best I could. Soon I again became a private in the British Army.

I now explored the colliery and its grounds. It lay on the outskirts of Wasmes, the village that we left on that fateful morning of August 24th, with all its buildings to the south of the pithead. These consisted of two blocks, one on each side of a road leading down to the village, and thirty feet above this ran a wooden footbridge connecting the upper floors of both. This structure also supported steam pipes, etc., running across from one building to the other. On the south side of the road stood a huge pair of iron gates, the only entrance to that part of the colliery, and just inside them was the boiler house, the beauty of its tall chimney marred by a shell-hole twenty feet above its base. This chimney was supposed at that time to be in imminent danger

of collapse, and everyone hurried past it. But their fears were
groundless. Later it withstood all attempts to pull it down
by means of a tractor, connected to it by a steel hawser, and
after that its shade became a favourite place for gossip and
love-making on the part of the hospital staff. On the north
side of the road stood the engine-room and the usual offices
connected with the business of a colliery.

I discovered that three buildings were being used to house
the wounded; one on the north side of the road for officers,
and two on the south side for N.C.O.s and men. Altogether
there were roughly forty British patients, the majority being
officers and N.C.O.s. There was one German, who belonged
to the famous Prussian Guard. The staff of the hospital consisted of two doctors, Dr Lecocq and an assistant, one certi-
fied nurse, and a score or so of voluntary helpers of both
sexes, the leader of this little band a certain M. Capiau, a
young Belgian engineer, who had been trained and educated
in England. He spoke English much better than most of the
Tommies under his care, and was always much in demand
as an interpreter.

There were only two patients able to get about on their
feet besides myself, Captain Taylor and Private Clark, both
of the Duke of Wellington's Regiment. They soon told me
that they were making preparations for a get-away, as they
understood it was possible to escape via Tournai, where
there was a gap in the German line. On hearing this I
begged to be allowed to go with them but, as arrangements
had only been made for two, it was really out of the question.
Further, as I was not yet able to walk very well, I might
have hindered their progress and so spoilt their chances.
Captain Taylor and Private Clark left the hospital one night
a little later, and successfully reached the British lines by
barge down the canal from Tournai to Ostend. Both of
them, I am sorry to say, were killed later at Hill 60.

For, so far the Germans had not yet discovered the hospital, and the patients hoped they never would, or at least not discover it before we were well enough to walk, and could disappear in the confusion which still reigned, like Captain Taylor and Private Clark. The Germans had not yet organised the territory they had occupied. This was not to be however. They walked in on September 3rd, and we British soldiers became prisoners of war, and the Belgian staff of the hospital were now compelled to work under their iron heel. So ended all our hopes for the time being of following in the footsteps of Captain Taylor and Private Clark. Later I learned that some small clinics in the district were never discovered by the Germans, and that all the patients in them were somehow got away.

The Germans now took control, and life in the hospital was never the same again. Nominal rolls of the wounded were rendered by the Belgians, but curiously enough the Germans never placed a guard on it. Whether this was due to shortage of men, or because they thought that no one there was capable of escaping, I do not know. Next day, too, they dumped a load of smashed-up rifles, collected from the surrounding battlefield, in the yard opposite my ward, an unpleasant reminder for us. They did not remain there long. Within a week the Belgians had 'souvenired' every piece worth taking away. M. Capiau also informed us that the Germans had drawn up stringent regulations, making him and another Belgian responsible for our safe custody; also for our food supply and medical necessaries.

As a matter of fact I saw few medical necessaries in the hospital ever, and there was always mighty little food to eat. The shortage of it in the village soon became acute and, after German requisitions had been met, there was very little left for anyone else, and we wounded were dependent on the charity of the local inhabitants. It was a matter of indifference to the Germans whether we starved or not. What little food we did get consisted chiefly of bread and stewed pears. Occasionally we were served with a concoction that the Belgians called *ragoût*, potato stew flavoured with bacon. The same piece must have been used over and over again as it could never be discovered in the pot! If one had money, one could buy eggs and chips at an estaminet just outside the gates. Money was scarce however, even among the officers. Further, it was soon put out of bounds.

Nevertheless the food situation was not really so bad as I have painted it perhaps. For occasionally we were given a few francs by benevolently inclined Belgians visiting the hospital, gifts that involved me in risking several visits to the estaminet after dark for eggs and chips for those who still wanted to eat. These were not many. Most of the poor fellows in my ward were gradually sinking and past all desire for food. The Prussian was, of course, in a different position. He was ordered all the luxuries he wanted.

I do not remember a single British patient in the colliery ever being examined or treated by a German doctor. Their treatment was left entirely in the hands of Dr Lecocq and his assistant, and they were handicapped from the start by scarcity of surgical equipment and insufficient medical supplies. Yet with scanty equipment, only really intended for first-aid work in a pithead emergency, they carried on, and their efforts were untiring. They performed many major operations, and did their best in the circumstances, but their labours never met with the success they deserved. In my ward alone there were eight cases of tetanus and, in spite of amputation in every one, only two survived.[1]

1. In 1914 the prevention of tetanus by inoculation with toxoid had not yet been introduced and the B.E.F., although protected against typhoid, were not protected against tetanus. The latter was a common complication of wounds and the mortality of the disease was always high.   *Editor*

One of these was an outstanding character, a little Cockney driver of the Royal Field Artillery. One moment he would be calling for a revolver to shoot the 'blasted' doctor who took off his leg; the next telling us what he would do when he got back to his favourite pub in the Old Kent Road. In spite of his suffering he had the will to live, and was well on the road to recovery when I left the hospital a few weeks later.

On the second day of the take-over the Germans nailed their flag to the underpart of the wooden footbridge so that it hung down over the road, plainly visible to all approaching from either direction. That same night it was ripped off, an outrage which brought a German staff officer post-haste to the scene and, in spite of the fact that there was not a single English patient there physically capable of climbing the bridge, we got the blame, and were threatened with punishment if it were not replaced immediately. So, as we could do nothing about it, some of us, it seemed, were in for a rough time. Next morning, however, the flag was once again in position, just as if nothing had happened. The perpetrators of the outrage (presumably Belgians) had 'played the game' by replacing it. This, no doubt, saved us from whatever punishment it was that we were to get.

Most of the wounded were in a pretty bad way, and hardly getting the attention they required from the voluntary staff. These were mostly young Belgians for whom the novelty of nursing was beginning to wear off. Nor did they much like the hard work it entailed. So, as I had nothing particular to do, I took upon myself the task of nursing orderly in the wards on my side of the colliery. As an army bandsman I had been trained in first aid and hospital nursing. So I was no novice at that kind of work, and while the voluntary staff were 'making eyes' at one another, I buzzed round and did their job. And I was happy doing it!

I now had a busy time changing dressings, replacing slipped bandages, and the other thousand and one things required of a nursing orderly. And I did exactly the same for the Prussian N.C.O. as I did for my own comrades. He had been badly wounded. A bullet had entered below his knee, passed through the joint, and come out above it, and he suffered great pain which, in my opinion, was aggravated by the Belgians. They handled him none too gently. He had great difficulty, too, in turning over, and sitting up in bed without help. This he rarely got from them. So, seeing his problem, I procured some rope and a piece of wood from the colliery store, and with these constructed a gadget that resembled a circus trapeze, which I fixed to an iron girder over his head. With the aid of this contrivance he was now able to turn over or sit up whenever he pleased. For this little service he was most grateful. Of course he could not tell me so in words, but he showed it in his eyes and actions. And we became good friends. If only it had been left to us, we could have ended hostilities between our two countries there and then!

The cigarettes which I was able to obtain from charity were of the cheapest brand made from strong black Belgian tobacco. Those ordered for the Prussian at the expense of the Belgians were Egyptian (Luxor brand). Just to show our friendship with one another however, we often exchanged cigarettes, and as he soon seemed to prefer my brand to his own, we started swopping packet for packet. This was much to my advantage. Until I left the hospital he never got to know that I could obtain two packets of Belgian black in exchange for one packet of his Egyptians at the estaminet. It was only by this bit of luck that I was sure of my cigarettes. He, being a German, had only to ask in order to receive. The Belgians dared not refuse him anything he wanted.

On the second day of my self-imposed task M. Capiau sent

for me, and asked if I would be willing to take over and look after a British officer, totally paralysed, whom the doctor had decided to remove from the officers' ward to a room by himself. The poor chap was delirious at night and kept all his brother officers awake. This, I told M. Capiau, I would be glad to do. So that evening I was duly installed in a small room, just large enough for two beds, with him. He belonged to the 2nd Battalion, the Duke of Wellington's Regiment, and was a tall gaunt man suffering from a shrapnel wound on the top of his head. This had fractured his skull and caused his paralysis. (If steel helmets had been worn in those days he would have escaped injury.) My first night with him was terrible. I was in and out of bed every few minutes, covering up imaginary lights, and tending to his needs, real and unreal. His screams must have been heard throughout my side of the colliery. I was more than glad when daylight came, he went to sleep, and I could get some too.

As he could not move at all I had to feed him, wash him, and keep changing his bed-linen. This last was my worst job. He was a hefty man and, being in a helpless state, was far too heavy for me to lift alone, and he hated the sight of the Belgian staff, and openly cursed them every time they came anywhere near him. So, as none of them would now help me, I had to invent a way of doing the job by myself, and soon thought of one. I placed our two beds about a foot apart with my pillow at the foot instead of at the head of mine. I would then gather him up in my arms, almost strangling him in the process, turn about quickly, and drop him on to my bed. Then, when his own bed was ready for him again, I would repeat the procedure by turning about in the opposite direction. This brought him back to his original position right way round on his own bed. After two or three days I became quite adept at this procedure.

Leaving his brother officers and coming in to the small

room with me hurt his feelings much. It was ever uppermost in his mind. He talked about it all day and raved about it all night. Again and again he asked to be allowed back but his request was never granted, and these repeated refusals began to play on his mind. Gradually his condition deteriorated, and my nights awake with him became nightmares. In his quieter moments, however, he would tell me about his family, and one day suddenly asked whether, if he died and I ever reached England, I would write to his sister and tell her 'all about it'. I promised this faithfully, and wrote down her address, a promise which I carried out within twenty-four hours of my getting home.

One morning, after an extremely bad night, he asked me to see M. Capiau with a view to his returning to the officers' ward. He felt that he would go mad if he had to remain where he was for even one more day.

'Tell Capiau that I promise not to make a sound, if only they will have me back.'

So I saw M. Capiau, who in turn asked the officers. But they replied that it was out of the question. Whereupon my patient lost all hope, and started to sob like a child. This was too much for me, and I decided that I must do my utmost to get him moved out of that room somehow. So, without telling anyone of my intentions, I went to the men's ward, and explained that he was fed up with being alone and wanted to come in with them. Would they have him, I said? And added that, if any man objected, he would get no further help from me! That clinched the matter. There were no objections, and I returned to my officer, and told him that the boys would welcome him in with them. Would he like to go? His answer came, pathetically:

'Yes, I would love that.'

So with M. Capiau's permission I got help, and moved him in with the men, and that night he slept like a top, his first untroubled sleep since he had been wounded. After that he remained quiet and contented until he passed away on the 17th September, dying in my arms as I was moving him from one bed to the other. His death was a happy release for him. He was buried in Wasmes German Cemetery, but in May 1918 his body was removed by the Germans to Hautege Military Cemetery.

We now had a German commandant in charge of the hospital who started transferring men to German prison camps as soon as they were fit to travel, but I missed him by accident on his first visit and, in so doing, missed my marching orders. I was the fittest of them all! So I warned M. Capiau that I would probably be sent to Germany after this man's next visit. But he had a plan to avoid it:

'By some lucky chance your regiment is not listed in the hospital records, or on the nominal roll in possession of the Commandant,' he said. 'So I will give you a Red Cross badge to sew on your tunic. Then I can record you as belonging to the Royal Army Medical Corps and, when the Commandant knows the work you are doing, you are bound to be kept on here until the end.'

On the face of it, this offer looked good, but I could foresee complications if I accepted it. What would happen when my particulars eventually reached England? Would the War Office disown me? Also, how would my wife be affected, if I transferred to the R.A.M.C.? So with these doubts in my mind I told M. Capiau that his was not a practical proposition, but that I had been doing a little thinking on my own and, in the job of looking after the delirious officer—this happened before he died—I had an opportunity, with his assistance, of dodging the Commandant for some time to come. I had expected trouble for not having been present at his first visit, and had already made a few judicious enquiries. He never counted the patients, it appeared, or checked his roll. So, assuming, as was pretty certain, that he would always visit the officers' ward first, that being the nearest to his office, I made a counter proposition. I explained to M. Capiau that the Commandant had not yet seen me and, if he, Capiau, agreed to do what I asked, there was no earthly reason why he ever should. My plan was for him to warn me of the Commandant's arrival so that I could then take up my bed and stow it in the store-room, and then keep clear of him myself until he had gone. Ten to one, if he saw no empty bed, and omitted to check the roll, he would never even suspect my existence!

M. Capiau thought this a sound scheme, and agreed to co-operate. In future he faithfully warned me in advance of every coming visit of the Commandant.

Except for that chap few Germans ever came inside our hospital, but one of these rare exceptions caused a little excitement outside our usual routine. He was a young officer, quite a boy in fact, who, as he walked round the wards, toyed with an automatic pistol in a truly aggressive manner, and the sneer on his face and his arrogant attitude so riled Lieutenant Sewell of my own regiment that, although he was dying of tetanus, we had great difficulty in restraining him from getting out of bed and throwing the bloody German out of the ward. Parties of reinforcements on their way to the front would, however, often pass by on the road through the colliery, and out of curiosity on one occasion I went down to the gates to watch them, only to be rewarded by being spat at by them in contempt. How they hated us English!

As time went on, what with my delirious officer dead, and many of my other patients dead or transferred to prison camps, I had increasingly little to do except, of course, continue to dodge the Commandant. And hunt for food! Supplies of that were dwindling steadily. One day I was peculiarly successful. While looking over a wall from the inside of the scrap-iron yard at the south end of the colliery, I spotted a shed full of potatoes which could easily be reached through a broken window. So, that night, and on many nights after that, I made a raid over the wall, and got sufficient for myself and a few others, took them to the stoke-hold of the gas retorts, which were just outside our ward, and baked them in the ashes under the fires, having first cultivated, of course, the friendship of the stoker on night duty by plying him with some of the cigarettes that I had made out of the favourable rate of exchange between the Prussian's and those sold by the estaminet.

The Prussian liked baked potatoes too, and he was always invited to take part in these feasts. But this apparent hospitality on my part had dual intent. First, he would be less likely to 'let on' as long as he was getting his share. Secondly, if I was caught, the fact that he was privy to my crime would at least lessen my punishment. As far as I could see the risk of being caught was really very small. For after each feast I always collected all the skins and burnt them in the stoke-hold, thereby destroying all evidence against me. My only real fear was being trapped in the act of scrounging them from the shed. Here my luck held until I left.

News of the war and of events in the outside world was very scarce, and even the Belgians did not seem to know what was going on outside occupied territory. The railways were all controlled by the Germans, and mainly used for rushing up war material and reinforcements to the Western Front. Trams that had connected towns and villages had long since ceased to run. Newspapers were censored, and editors only allowed to print such copy as was authorised by the Germans, mainly news of German victories of course. Most Belgians were forced to travel to work on foot, as owners of horse-drawn vehicles had to obtain permits before they

could carry passengers. No civilian was allowed abroad between 8 p.m. and 6 a.m. without a permit. Indeed, almost
every day or so, it seemed, some new order was issued restrict-
ing still further the freedom of the civilian population, the
onus for carrying out orders of this kind being placed on the
shoulders of the unhappy local authorities. Such was the
burden of the German yoke. Almost everything reasonable
was *verboten*.

In the absence of authentic news rumour was always rife.
One day we would hear that the Russian steam-roller had
arrived at Berlin, and that the city was in flames; the next
that all British prisoners were being shot before they reached
Germany. This was not very cheering for us! And so it went
on day after day, nothing certain, everything always in the
air, most of these rumours being circulated by Belgians and
their wives visiting the hospital. Many of these 'adopted' a
particular patient who happened to take their fancy, and
naturally it was interesting and amusing to watch visitors
and patients endeavouring to understand one another by
signs, punctuated by vocal interjections such as '*Oui*' and
'*Non compris*', in most cases the patient's limit in respect of
his knowledge of the French language. Nevertheless, the
degree of understanding at which they arrived by such
methods was truly remarkable. Not being a bed patient myself, and therefore either absent or working during visiting
hours, I never became friendly with any particular visitor.
On the other hand, I always shared any of the good things
that they left behind.

October 22nd proved my unlucky day. The Commandant,
contrary to his usual routine, checked his list and counted the
patients, found that he was one short, and, as he could not
see a vacant bed, naturally asked M. Capiau where I slept.
This caught him unawares and, for the moment, he was at a
loss for an answer, but after some hesitation explained that I

Hospital and colliery staff and British patients: a picture taken at the Hornu-Wasmes coal mine soon after the battle. Not all the people are identifiable. In the front row the second figure from the left is Dr Lecocq and the figure second from the right is Dr Huart. In the second row the first five figures from right to left are M. Herman Capiau, M. Daubresse (director of the brewery), M. Barbier (engineer), Mme Barbier and an engineer of the mine.

No...   Army Form B 104—82.
(If replying, please quote above No.)

.... Record Office,

.... Station.

.................../....... 10 ..., 191 4.

S<small>IR</small>, Madam,

It is my painful duty to inform you that a report has this day been received from the War Office notifying the death of (No.) 7555 (Rank) Private (Name) Henry Walter Beaumont (Regiment) Rl West Kent Regt which occurred at .... on the 24th of August 1914, and I am to express to you the sympathy and regret of the Army Council at your loss. The cause of death was Killed in action

Any application you may wish to make regarding the late soldier's effects should be addressed to " The Secretary, War Office, Whitehall, London, S.W.," and marked on the outside, " Deceased Soldiers' Effects."

I am,

S<small>IR</small>, Madam,

Your obedient Servant,

WM Peake

Captain for Colonel,
I C Infantry Records, Hounslow.
Officer in charge of Records

(K11219)   Wt W2537—200,000—8/14.   W. & Co., Ltd.

The official notification of my death

had rendered valuable assistance nursing the patients at night after the voluntary staff had gone home, and that he thought I slept in the store-room during the day. As this information was news to the Commandant he demanded to be taken to the store-room. There he found my bed but did not find me!

He now began to suspect that there was something fishy about this, and returned to the ward to question the Prussian N.C.O. He confirmed that I did all the night nursing, and added that I had done more for him than anyone else in the whole hospital. But the Commandant was now thoroughly rattled, and ordered M. Capiau to search the colliery and, when he had found me, to bring me to his office without delay. Of course, M. Capiau knew where I was, realised that the game was up, and did what he was told. So, in less than five minutes, I was 'on the mat' in the office. The Commandant's face was a picture to behold. I needed no telling that I was 'in the soup'. He leapt up from his chair, and, baring his yellow teeth, commenced firing questions at me in very fair English with the precision and rapidity of a machine gun:

'Who are you? I've never seen *you* before.'

I replied by giving him my name and regimental particulars, which he checked by his list, remarking that, according to it, I had no regiment, although he would take my word in respect of that. He next asked:

'How long have you been here, and why have you been absent from the ward on every one of my inspections?'

My reply to the first part of his question was that I entered the hospital on August 26th; to the second, the first excuse that came into my head, namely, that I was fond of fresh air and spent most of the day in the grounds, and that, as his visits were irregular, it was only a coincidence that I had been absent from the ward during his inspections. This last remark

E

put the finishing touch to his ruffled temper. Almost choked by the three-inch collar of his tunic, he exploded:

'Fresh air! Fresh air!' he yelled. 'I'll send you to Stettin-on-Oder. You'll get far more fresh air than you want there.'

Innocently I asked where this place was, at which he looked at me in utter disgust, but, before he could reply, M. Capiau tried to calm him down by explaining what good work I had done in the hospital. He was not to be side-tracked however, and told M. Capiau that any good work that I might have done was no excuse whatever for my outrageous conduct. Further, he accused Capiau of being in league with me, and looking at him remarked:

'You say he works all night and sleeps in the store-room by day. He says he spends his days in the grounds. You are both damned liars.'

With these words he closed the interview, and ordered M. Capiau to take the 'English swine' away, adding that he would report the matter to higher authority with a recommendation as to the punishment. This, he hoped, would be inflicted on both of us at his next visit. So far as I was concerned his next visit was too late. The bird had flown already!

4

Flight

On leaving the office M. Capiau told me not to worry about what the Commandant had said. The worst that could happen would be a few days' imprisonment for us both. Nevertheless, I made up my mind there and then that I was never going to Stettin-on-Oder, and next day sounded M. Capiau, and some of the Belgian staff, who understood a little English, on the possibilities of escaping. But they were much too afraid of the consequences to themselves if I did that, and refused to give me either any information or any help. In fact, by mentioning the subject to them, I think I did myself much more harm than good. My movements about the colliery were very carefully watched after that.

The following night I felt thoroughly depressed, really fed up in fact, and ready to adopt any mad scheme of escape that might come along, however risky. Indeed, I felt so fed up that on entering the ward I exclaimed aloud, so that everyone could hear: 'I'd clear out of this bloody place straight away if I saw a chance.' Whereupon Lance-Corporal A. Heath, of my own regiment, called me across to his bed, and when out of hearing of the others, asked me in a whisper if I really meant what I had just said. I assured him that I did indeed. He then told me that he had a plan to get away, and that, as soon as the other patients had settled down for the night, he would tell me all about it.

Heath was one of our casualties in the Place du Wasmes

in the early morning of August 24th. He had just borrowed a bucket from one of the cottagers nearby, and was indulging in a much-needed wash at the village pump, when the Germans started shelling. The owner of the bucket, a woman, immediately rushed out to get it. Heath pushed her back into the cottage for safety, returned to the pump himself, refilled it, and handed it back to her, and the woman had only just closed her door when a shell exploded and Heath got hit. He was picked up at once by a chemist named Caliau, who gave him first aid, and then carried him to the colliery hospital. That was before the Germans actually entered the village.

So I bustled round that night early, and made all my patients comfortable and, as soon as most of them seemed asleep, crept over to Heath to learn about his plan. He had become very friendly, he told me, with a Belgian and his wife, named Neusy. They were regular visitors to the hospital, and had offered to take care of him, and arrange for him to leave the country somehow, if he could manage to get to their house; and he now showed me a rough map of the roads leading to it which they had given him drawn on a sheet of notepaper. At the top was written: '2nd house, iron railings, the Rue Calvier.' How far was it, I asked, from the colliery to the Rue Calvier? Heath said that, as far as he had been able to gather, it was only about four miles, but knowing that Heath had been shot through the thigh, I naturally wondered how he expected to be able to walk four miles. His reply staggered me:

'Ah, old man, that's the point. Now, look! This is the position as I see it. You want to get away, and have nowhere to go. I have somewhere to go, and can't get away, because I can't walk. So, if we both go, you'll have to carry me,' adding that he knew it was a bold proposition, but would I do it?

Heath weighed, I estimated, between ten and eleven stone, and I knew that I was taking on a tough job, but, given sufficient start, I was confident of my ability to carry him that distance. I would do it, even if it meant finishing on my knees. It was the only plan of any kind that offered, and, if we failed, it would be better to have tried and failed than never to have tried at all.

On one point only was I doubtful. Would the Neusys be prepared to do the same for me as they had promised to do for him? He assured me that he was quite certain that they would, and jokingly remarked: 'If not, old man, you will be at liberty to carry me back again!' This comment clinched it, and we grasped each other's hand to seal a bargain that led us to embark on a series of adventures which, had we known what they were to be, might well have deterred me.

Heath was already in possession of a blue boiler suit on loan from the colliery. This he wore to save his uniform while getting about the ward on crutches, and it would now be an excellent disguise in which to get away, as it was the common dress worn by the miners in the village, and would excite no suspicion among the Germans while we were on the move. But I, too, had to get hold of civvies of some kind somehow. The question was how. I had not given the stoker cigarettes and cultivated his friendship for nothing however. Rather, under the guise of that, I had watched his habits very carefully with a view to possible eventualities. I knew that he came on duty at 6 p.m. every evening in an ordinary suit; also that a few minutes after his arrival he changed into dungarees which he took from a peg behind the stokehold door where they hung. He would then work until about 3 a.m. the next morning, by which time he had filled up the retorts for the last time during his tour of duty, and would then find a convenient spot and fall off to sleep until his relief came on at 6 a.m. So with a bit of luck that civvy suit of his was mine for the taking. And I knew it fitted me. I had already tried on the coat while he was sleeping!

As to the time and date of our escape we decided to wait until after the Neusys' next visit. We wanted to let them know that two of us were coming!

In the meantime I got Heath up as much as I could, and made him practise walking with two sticks that I had scrounged for the purpose, in case I proved unable to carry him all the way. No doubt he would have been much more at home on his crutches, but if he took them, and he was forced to use them, they would leave an indelible trail in the soft earth, making it easy for any pursuers to track us. So, in the circumstances, sticks it had to be! But I felt genuinely sorry for him as I watched him gallantly walking up and down the ward with the aid of those damned sticks. I could see by his face that every step hurt him, but he stuck it until he almost collapsed, and in case anyone was suspicious I remarked, for the benefit of all and sundry, that he had to learn to walk, as he would soon be going to Germany. One patient unfortunately commented, 'Well, why not let them carry him?' None guessed his real intentions.

Our plans for escape were now cut and dried, and we anxiously awaited the next visit of the Neusys. On October 25th I got a rude shock however. M. Capiau sent for me, and told me that he had instructions that I was to be in readiness to proceed to Germany under escort at 10 a.m. next morning! This was a shock indeed but, without letting either my voice or my face betray my feelings, I replied:

'All right, M. Capiau, I'll be ready then.'

Once out of the office I lost no time in getting back to the ward to break this startling news to Heath. Clearly it was now or never, and we decided to make it now and push off at 4 a.m. the following morning. There was no other option, and we could not get away before that, of course, as I had still to get my suit of civvies. Heath now insisted that, as all the hard work next day was to be done by me, I should go to bed as usual while he kept awake to call me at 3.45 a.m. So I made everyone comfortable, I hoped for the last time, and then took Heath's two sticks and hid them behind the iron gates. Everything was now in readiness for zero hour. Then I went to bed.

Exactly at 3.45 Heath came over to give me a shake. This was quite unnecessary. I had not slept a wink. My brain had been far too active, thinking and wondering how the great adventure would end, to permit of that. And another patient had been lying awake besides us two. This was the Prussian who, being in much pain, slept badly. His leg should have been amputated but he had refused to let the Belgian doctors touch it and his own nationals hardly seemed to care whether he lived or died. He now gazed down the ward in our direction, and I was certain that he guessed what we were up to. I knew that he regarded me as a friend, but I was not quite sure what he would do when he actually saw us go.

Heath quickly got into his boiler suit, and then quietly left the ward on his crutches. I saw him clear of it, and then crept cautiously towards the stokehold where, after a little reconnaissance, I found the stoker fast asleep, as I had expected, and by the pleasant look on his face, dreaming about the end of the war or something else equally pleasant. Quickly I claimed his suit, and tiptoed to the store-room to put it on. This accomplished, I went through all his pockets, and found a red handkerchief and numerous other articles such as any average man carries about with him. These I tied up in it and, returning to the stokehold, placed it on the peg from which I had taken his suit. I did not want to rob him of more than was necessary, and left him sleeping peacefully, oblivious to the extraordinary events taking place around him.

For the second time in a brief period I had now donned civilian clothes which, if things went wrong, would place me in a precarious position with either friend or foe. But I still retained two very old friends in my army boots. Civilian boots were at a premium, and very difficult to obtain, and the Belgian working class wore sabots, which were not quite the things to choose to escape in. They are difficult to walk far in and much too noisy on cobbles.

I was now ready to join Heath at the gate, but before doing so was overcome by a desire to have one last look at the ward where I had spent so many days among my wounded comrades and, as I rashly peeped through the door, I was spotted by the Prussian. He beckoned me to come in. Inwardly I cursed myself for being such a sentimental idiot, and now I hesitated to present myself to him dressed as a civilian at four o'clock in the morning. He would be bound to see that I was off. I hesitated, I say, whether to go in or not, but it was the last request that I could grant him. Instinctively, I trusted him.

He gave me the usual sign to help him turn over, and while doing so, a strange thing happened. He clung to my hand like a child and, as he looked into my face, his eyes told me all I wanted to know. I could see that, so far as he was concerned, Heath and I had nothing whatever to fear. Then, raising himself on one elbow, he reached over and opened his locker from which he extracted his last packet of cigarettes and a bottle of red wine. These he pressed me to take. One more handshake, and I left the ward, but as I passed out through the door, I turned and saw him feebly waving me goodbye. Then he placed his finger on his lips, as a sign that he at least would keep his mouth shut. I returned his gesture of farewell. Then I was gone, and at that moment an almost unbelievable friendship ended, humanity triumphant over hatred.

Grasping that bottle of wine by the neck I joined Heath at the gates, who remarked that I had been 'a devil of a time', and wanted to know 'what the hell' I had been doing. I replied that I had just been saying goodbye to the Prussian, 'that's all'. Whereupon, glancing at the way in which I was holding the bottle, he exclaimed, 'Good Lord! You haven't done him in, have you?' 'He was too good a pal for me to harm him,' I said, and explained just what had happened. Heath agreed it was a rather wonderful thing in the circumstances to have had a German for a pal, and suggested that we opened the bottle forthwith to drink to his speedy recovery. This we did immediately.

Then, without further delay, I retrieved Heath's two sticks from their hiding-place behind the gates, and handed them to him in exchange for his crutches. These I hid in a stack of iron gas mains. Then, with shaking hands, I unbolted the gates, and silently opened them sufficiently wide for us to pass through and, closing them behind us, had the strage feeling of being on the threshold of a great adventure. Whether I was nervous or excited I could not tell. But I was definitely far from normal at that moment.

For a few seconds we stood and watched the lighted windows of the buildings on the other side of the road for any sign of movement of the staff on duty in the officers' ward but, seeing none, started to creep along, like two thieves, hugging the wall of the building on the south side of the road until we were clear of the lighted windows. We did not hear a sound, and five minutes later left the colliery road by turning right, according to Neusy's map. With Heath limping along on his sticks our progress was tediously slow, and before we had travelled two hundred yards I could tell that he was in a very bad way. The exertion was too much for his strength. So, raising him on my shoulders, pick-a-back style, I carried him until we came to a fork. This meant studying the map, and I was also very glad of the excuse for a rest. Heath had proved much heavier to carry than I had anticipated. Out now came a box of matches; the old-fashioned paraffin Tandstickers with red heads dipped in sulphur which twinkled like a star and then nearly gassed the holder before they burst into flame. They were known in the heyday of their existence as 'Wait-a-Minutes'. That night they served their purpose.

Having now got 'on course', I picked up Heath again, and we continued our journey. But it did not matter how I carried him. To do so at all I was almost bound to grasp his painful leg, and for him the journey must have been little short of hell. Several times I heard him groan, and apologised for causing him so much pain. But he would never admit it. He just said, 'That's all right, old man. Carry on.' Further, as time went on, he seemed to become heavier and heavier. So our stages became correspondingly shorter and shorter; our rests more and more frequent and longer and longer. Occasionally he tried to walk for a bit. But he could never walk for long.

Twice that morning on that hectic journey we met peasants on their way to work. Each time I dropped Heath to his feet, and he immediately took to his sticks and jabbered to me in some imaginary language of his own for the benefit of those passers-by. I never quite gathered his idea in doing this. I suppose he thought it would lull suspicion. It invariably created just the opposite effect. Each time they stopped and stared at us open-mouthed, probably thinking us escaping lunatics.

Eventually, after two hours of twisting and turning, along lanes and tracks leading across cultivated land, we arrived at what we believed to be one end of the Rue Calvier in the village of Petit Wasmes. Day was breaking, and no one was more relieved than I to think that we had at last reached our objective. It had been a terrible journey. I only trusted now that our map was correct, and that we had read it right, but street names are not inscribed on the walls of Belgian villages for the benefit of strangers, and we did not know for certain whether we were right or not. I was exhausted, and could not have carried, even supported, Heath much further. As it was we had to work our way slowly up the street, looking for 'the second house with the iron railings'. This to our relief we soon found—we had read our map right—but, like all the others in the street, it showed no signs of life. The Neusys were not expecting visitors at that hour in the morning.

We first tried the iron gate at the front entrance to their house which was semi-detached. It was locked. Then I went down an alley between two brick walls six feet high leading to a back entrance, this alley being blocked at about half the depth of the house by a wooden door flush with the top of the walls. It was locked too. This of course was understandable. We had forgotten for the moment that, as the result of our premature flight, we had been unable to warn the Neusys of our coming. So I now tugged with increasing fury at the bell on the front gate without response of any kind. Then with Heath's help I scaled the wall, and knocked on the front door of the house. Still I got no reply. How those people could sleep! And I was afraid to knock too hard lest I roused their neighbours who we were most anxious should not witness our arrival. At length and in despair I tried the well-known method of throwing gravel at the bedroom window.

Suddenly this was thrown up, and out popped a head covered with black curly hair to see what all the rumpus was about. It was Neusy! He stared at me for a moment. But he did not recognise me, and still half asleep muttered something that I did not understand. Heath, who was still outside the railings, coughed to attract his attention. In this he was successful. The look on Neusy's face changed from wonderment to delight, and turning to someone in the room, presumably his wife, he literally shouted, '*Artude! Artude!*', the French version of Arthur, Heath's own Christian name.

In a few moments, still wearing his nightshirt, Neusy was down unlocking the gate to let us in, both to be hugged and kissed, both by him and by his wife. This demonstration of affection to me, a complete stranger, was somewhat surprising and certainly embarrassing. At that time I was not yet familiar with the customs of the Belgian people.

Within a few minutes a fire was kindled, and breakfast in course of preparation, and while Neusy and his wife retired to get properly dressed, Heath and I watched the kettle boil, and were soon greeted by a boy of eleven, Robert, Neusy's only child.

Conversation during breakfast was difficult and slow, mutual understanding only being possible by signs, such as Madame Neusy exhibiting her wedding ring, then linking arms with her husband, and then taking my left hand and touching its third finger. This, I gathered, was an enquiry as to whether I was married or not. That question settled, it was followed by enquiries as to how many children I had, signified by Mme Neusy stretching out her arm horizontally and raising it by intervals. She then held up her fingers until she obtained the required number. All this took time, but it was surprising how many questions were asked and how many answered by these methods. Certainly any misgiving on my part as to whether Neusy would take me in as well as Heath soon faded away. These people, I could see, were big-hearted enough to have taken a dozen British soldiers in, if circumstances had demanded that they should. Indeed, although I had only known the Neusys for two hours, I already felt quite at home and comfortable, and well prepared to settle down under their roof until Heath had recovered sufficiently to walk, and arrangements could be made for both of us to get to Holland.

My hopes were soon dashed. At about 9 a.m. there was a sudden vigorous pull at the bell from the gate at the side entrance which made us jump. Who was it at that hour? Of course I guessed at once. As soon as the hospital had found out that we were missing, knowing that Heath had had many visits from the Neusys, someone would certainly be sent to find out if they knew anything about us. We might have thought of that!

Mme Neusy quickly shoved us behind some thick curtains, while her husband went and unlocked the back gate to deal with the visitor and, as soon as I heard his voice, I recognised it as belonging to one of the Belgian officials at the hospital. He was asking questions. Before long they were in an excited and heated argument. Of course I could not understand a word of what they said, but it was obvious that it must be about our escape, and yet that Belgian left, to our extreme relief, after a while without ever even coming in. Neusy had worked wonders, and when I was able to speak a little French, I learned that he had bluffed him by actually inviting him to come in and search the house! I also learned that he had been sent by a colonel, a patient in the hospital, with a message to the effect that, if we did not return at once, he would tell the Germans. Fortunately, not being able to understand French at this time, we did not get, and therefore could not have been blamed for disobeying, his order. At the same time, had we understood it, I do not honestly think that we would have obeyed it. We had burned our boats behind us. We would have needed a very great deal of persuading to make us go back.[1]

1. This episode raises a question in military law. A soldier is bound to obey any order given by an officer *unless* under the circumstances the execution of it would contravene the purpose for which it was intended, or the officer was not in a fit state to give it. In short, he is not expected to obey blindly but to understand his orders, and in certain circumstances exercise his judgement. On the other hand, a soldier's duty, if captured by the enemy, is to escape, if he can, and rejoin his regiment. The Colonel gave this order—whether he was in a fit condition as a wounded and sick man to give it is by no means certain—to avoid reprisals on the hospital. Beaumont escaped in order to avoid being sent to Germany as a prisoner and in the hope of being able to rejoin his unit. Had the case come to court martial, Beaumont's defence could have pointed to the consequences of his disobedience. He did succeed in rejoining his unit, and there were no serious reprisals on the hospital.   *Editor*

5

Hiding in the wood

AFTER this unwelcome visitor had left Neusy had a long discussion with his wife. She seemed a little scared at the turn events had taken but he soon decided what was to be done in the circumstances. He inspected my civilian rig-out, and made me exchange my army boots for a pair of civilian ones. So at last I lost those old friends to which I had stuck through thick and thin. (They were taken to the bottom of the garden and buried without ceremony of any kind!) Neusy also produced a soft collar and a felt hat for me, and at 9.30 a.m. it became clear that I was expected to leave the house with the boy Robert and his little dog, Follett, a small curly haired terrier. And leave it, too, for an unknown destination!

On and on we walked, the boy, I, and the dog, avoiding habitations of all kinds, and by devious tracks and by-ways, until after an hour and a half without an incident of any kind we came in sight of some woods. These I guessed were our objective. Thirty minutes later we reached a spot deep in them far away from any path that a chance pedestrian might take. Here Robert made me understand that I was to stay and, leaving me Follett for company, made off, presumably to return home.

Not knowing exactly what was expected of me now, or what was going to happen next, and alone with my thoughts, I could not help thinking that so far our escape had not been the success we had hoped. I even seriously began to doubt

whether we had really been wise in making the attempt at
all. I was also anxious to know what had happened to Heath.
What were the Neusys going to do with him? I knew that his
exertions that morning had caused him a great deal of pain,
and I doubted whether he was capable of walking again that
day. Indeed, I doubted whether he would be able to walk at
all for many weeks to come.

In the afternoon Mme Neusy turned up, however, bringing me food and coffee, but although she did her level best to
tell me all she could, except for the fact that I had to stay
put just where I was, I gained no information about Heath
or about anything else whatever. Then with tears in her
eyes, knowing that she had failed in this respect, she bade
me *au revoir* and departed, taking the dog, which evidently
preferred the company of his mistress to mine, with her.

I devoutly wished that Heath had been with me during her
visit. He was far more experienced in talking with them by
signs, and could grasp their meaning much quicker than I
could. The trouble was that I did not know how long I was
really expected to stay where I was. Was it just for a day, or
for a week, or for what? And what was going to happen after
that? I waited as patiently as I could but, as the afternoon
wore on, and I saw the sun slowly sinking behind the trees,
I naturally began to think that it really was time that someone turned up about something. But no one turned up. So I
began to feel uneasy, and eventually left my hiding place,
and followed a path leading out of the wood. On this I met a
few stray pedestrians who greeted me with the customary
'*Bon jour*'. This politeness I tried to return in the language.
My pronunciation was so bad, however, that it clearly made
them suspicious. It must have been obvious to them that I
was a foreigner. So, when the next pedestrian greeted me in
the same way, I did not answer. But this apparent display
of bad manners had the effect of inviting curiosity. It was

hopeless! In despair I made off into the undergrowth, away from the tracks of man altogether, until I got clear of the wood.

I reached the open with no definite plan of action but, noticing a slag-heap a short distance away, I turned my steps towards it, and arriving at its base slowly climbed to the top in order to get my bearings and to think out some kind of plan for the morrow. There I sat for a while, watching the sun setting like a golden ball against the gathering twilight. Then I decided that on the morrow I would go in that direction, i.e. west, my only reason for this decision being that the British must be in that direction.

Having decided on this daft plan—had I acted on it I would have marched straight into German hands—I now started to look round for some shelter for the night and, as I did so, caught sight in the failing light of a tiny spot of white darting in and out of the edge of the wood. I could not make up my mind what it was at first. Then I suddenly realised that it was a dog, and soon saw that it was accompanied by, or rather accompanied, a man and a woman. Then in a flash it dawned on me. The dog was Follett! The man and woman were the Neusys, looking for me! God, what a bloody fool I had been to get into a panic, and leave the wood, and make half-baked plans of my own, thinking they had let me down!

I lost no time in getting to them. They seemed just as pleased to see me as I was pleased to see them, and as we walked along together they had a great deal to say to me, of which I did not understand a word, although from the tone of their voices it was perfectly clear that I was being severely 'told off' for disobeying their orders. I should have stayed where I was put. A few minutes later, too, I was with Heath himself. He had been hidden in a deep hole covered over with branches and undergrowth. The Neusys, of course,

F

tried to explain what was in their minds, but in the darkness, without being able to make signs, they just could not get anything across to us. We, on our part, just could not understand what they were trying to get at. Then Neusy had a bright idea. Pulling a box of matches, a pencil and a piece of paper from his pocket, he started to draw. In the centre he drew some trees. Then on one side of them he drew some Germans. Then on the other side of them he drew some gendarmes. His was a crude sketch, but we were there in a flash! It was sufficient to tell us that both the German and the Belgian police were out searching for us. Seeing that we understood at last Neusy was greatly relieved and, after giving us some cigarettes and matches, he and his wife said good night and departed on their way.

Heath now told me that he left the Rue Calvier about half an hour after me, and travelled to the wood in the bottom of a donkey cart covered over with sacks and old clothes. The cart was driven by an old man whose business was collecting rags and bones. It was good to be together again, he said, but he also said that he felt very rough, and that his leg was extremely painful.

I shall never forget the nights that Heath and I spent in those woods, lying on the damp ground, thinly clad as we were, and without covering of any kind. It was the end of October and bitterly cold. The damp seemed to creep into our very bones. Neither of us could sleep, and the sound of the wind whistling and moaning through the trees got on both our nerves. Each night seemed like an eternity. We were always thankful when morning came. For me at least this meant a little exercise and some hope of getting warm again. But for Heath, poor fellow, it meant no let-up. He just had to go on lying where he was, far too weak to stand or to use his legs. It was bad for me. For Heath it must have been terrible.

After breakfasting on our first morning, off the rations that the Neusys had brought the night before, I collected all the dead leaves I could find in the immediate vicinity of our hiding-place, and filled up the hole with them in order to make Heath a bit more comfortable if I could. This job done he declared that his bed was now as good as any spring mattress, and that the only other thing needed to make it perfect in fact was a couple of good old British Army blankets!

We now tried to think out what to do while in hiding like this. One point was clear. We could rely on the Neusys absolutely for our food, and also to get us away when the hue and cry after us had died down. On the other hand, we realised that we were in great danger from search parties, and that we would always have to keep a very sharp look-out during daylight or we would get caught. Finally we decided that there was no alternative to Heath remaining in the hole while I watched and patrolled the woods at intervals.

On my first patrol I discovered that the wood was approximately a mile in breadth and three-quarters of a mile in depth, and that it ran practically parallel with the French frontier. In the distance away to the south-east lay a large town, which I judged to be Maubeuge, and at points where tracks or roads crossed the frontier I could see German soldiers on patrol and French gendarmes. Both appeared to be checking the papers of people crossing the frontier from either direction. The main tracks through the wood itself were littered with guns, limbers and wagons, most of them British and smashed beyond repair. I searched among them, but searched in vain, in the hope of finding something useful for our bed or materials out of which to make some sort of a roof over our heads.

During the day I saw several small German patrols on the move and watched them from under cover. None of them appeared to be engaged in anything but ordinary routine duties, and I did not think that they were specifically looking for us. Only two actually came anywhere near the wood. These passed through it in the direction of France. Presumably they were reliefs for frontier duty. I made one find that day: a nearby spring of clear fresh water.

Every hour I returned to Heath to report what I had seen, and to cheer him up. Each time I did so from a different direction. I was most anxious to avoid making a beaten track which could be followed to our hiding-place.

When it began to get dark I came off duty, and joined him in the hole where we lay and smoked in silence. We expected a visit from the Neusys, and at about eight o'clock heard the rustle of approaching footsteps through the dead leaves, and sure enough Mme Neusy appeared with our rations for the next day. She was alone this time and, as conversation was impossible in the dark, she did not stay long. She soon bade us good night and, as she was moving off, I took her by the arm and led her out of the wood in an entirely different direction from that by which she had come into it. I was determined that, if she had been watched on arrival, no one should see her depart. Some weeks later I learnt that, not understanding my motive, my conduct that night had rather frightened her at first. Only when she reached the road in safety did she understand why I had led her deeper into the wood, and in apparently the wrong direction.

After another sleepless night I commenced my second day's patrol, determined to beg, borrow or steal something of some kind for a covering to keep us a little warmer at night. I soon thought I had been lucky. During the morning I discovered a barn belonging to a farm on the eastern side of the wood in which, from under cover of the trees, I could see some empty sacks and a heap of straw. These I ear-marked in my mind for attention after dark. It was clearly out of the question to try to purloin anything during daylight. So, that night, full of hope, I made my way to the barn to carry out a raid, but when within thirty yards of it I got a rude shock. The place suddenly became alive with dogs, which kicked up such a din that they brought the owner out with a lantern to see what all the noise was about. So, waiting until he had returned to the house, and all had become quiet again, and thinking that the dogs were chained up, I tried reaching my objective from the opposite direction. Now to my dismay I discovered that they were loose. They were probably also fierce, and it was out of the question to risk trying again. Instead, sadly disappointed, and hating all dogs for the first time in my life, I returned to Heath to report failure, and to to endure another bitterly cold and sleepless night listening to the wind.

Before long that wood had become an open book to me. I was familiar with every track, knowing whence it came and whither it led, and could find my way back to our hiding hole from any direction. Indeed, I now knew it so well that on our fourth day in it I was a little careless. Just before midday I was walking along one of the main tracks when, on turning a bend, I suddenly saw a party of Germans coming towards me. My mind must have wandered off my job for the moment, but there it was, and I had to make it up at once as to what was best to do. At first I thought of turning about, and making a bolt for it, but quickly realised that such an action would only arouse their suspicion. So I resolved to go boldly forward and chance my luck. Maybe they were not looking for us, and would merely think that I was some villager. This surmise proved correct. As I stepped aside to let them pass, the N.C.O. in charge acknowledged my salute, and merely bade me '*Guten tag*'. This sudden encounter came as a great shock to me however, and temporarily upset my nerve, making my heart jump. After giving the patrol time to get well round the next bed, however, I followed them cautiously until I was satisfied that they were well clear of our immediate vicinity.

Three nights of exposure to the elements did not improve Heath's condition, and in our hurried escape we had forgotten one thing. This was a supply of dressings. Not that dressings were plentiful at the hospital, but had we foreseen our present predicament, we could have commandeered enough for his needs for at least a few days. As it was, the one Heath had on his wound when we escaped had now been turned, split and re-turned until it was filthy, and had long since ceased to be of any real use at all. Further, his wound had gone septic, was discharging freely, and now needed repeated fresh dressings. He was one of those obstinate fellows however who would never complain and, when I suggested tearing up my shirt in order to make them, he simply would not hear of it.

'Don't do that. God knows you have got little enough to keep you warm as it is.'

In despair I sat with my head between my hands, sorely worried about Heath. I racked my brains to think of something that could be used to make do as a dressing, but in vain, and then, as I sat there I must have dozed off for a few moments. For I had a dream that gave me a wonderful idea. In it I saw myself dressing Heath's wound with leaves which had fallen from the trees around us! Then I woke up with a start. Whereupon, without saying anything to him, lest he ridiculed my idea, I walked away out of his sight, and collected all the largest and cleanest leaves that I could find, and washed them thoroughly in the spring. Then, returning to Heath, I made them up into a pad, and bound it tightly on his wound. Whether this novel form of dressing really did him good I cannot say, but he declared that leaves had a wonderfully soothing effect, and that he suffered less after I had done it. Further, I could now change the dressings on his wound as often as was necessary.

In spite of everything I tried to do, as these miserable days wore on, eventually Heath caught a chill. Before long this developed into bronchitis. Soon he had lost all interest in food, and only asked for water. Indeed, it was obvious now that he could not stand many more nights of this awful exposure, and so far as I could see the only way to get help was by giving ourselves up to the Germans. At first I thought of doing this on my own without telling him. But I was glad that I did not. When I did suggest it, he flatly refused to agree to anything of the kind. He would 'sooner die where he was,' he said, 'than surrender to those bastards'. And I knew it was quite useless to argue with him. He always meant every word he said, and his courage and determination put new heart into me. Nevertheless, the following morning, our tenth day in the wood, his condition was pitiful. His eyes were sunken and glaring, his face flushed, his skin bathed in sweat. He must have had a very high temperature, and again I had to put the suggestion to him that we should give ourselves up. Again he refused to hear of it.

That night he seemed to lapse into a semi-conscious state and refused even water. The dilemma I was in was now terrible. I simply did not know what to do for the best. It was my duty to try to save his life at all costs, even at the price of surrendering ourselves to the Germans and taking the risk of being shot. In the end I decided to postpone the final decision until the next morning. For Madame Neusy had visited us every single night since the first day of our escape, although this meant a walk of thirteen miles every day. No doubt she would turn up at about eight o'clock that evening as usual with our rations. No words of mine can ever adequately describe my admiration for this frail little woman who risked her life to befriend two British soldiers that she hardly knew!

She came as usual and, as I saw her clear of the wood that night, I went with her down the road and, as we walked along, tried my level best to make her realise Heath's condition. But she still could not understand me. I could not make her see it. Half a mile down the road however was an estaminet and, as we approached it, I suddenly decided to take a great risk. Before she realised what I was doing, I had seized her by the arm and pulled her inside, closing the door behind me firmly. I knew I was taking a great risk. At that time of night in such a spot it might well be like entering a village pub in England. It might well be crowded. Everyone present would realise that we were strangers, and immediately sit up and take notice. But I was lucky. There were only two customers there besides the landlord.

Madame Neusy ordered drinks, and we retired to a table in a far corner of the room. There I tried desperately to explain to her about Heath by means of signs and drawings on the sanded floor. Gradually she began to realise at last that I wanted to convey something really serious to her. But for the life of me I could not get her to grasp my meaning yet. My luck was in that night however. One of the customers, who had been watching us closely, came over and spoke to Madame Neusy, and she told him that I was English, and he turned out to be a seaman and a brother of the proprietor. (Owing to the war his ship was laid up.) Further, he could speak a little English, and it did not take me long to explain to Madame through him that I thought my friend was dying. A few moments later the seaman and I set off with a shutter, removed from the estaminet window, as a stretcher, and a cushion as a pillow, in the direction of the woods in order to bring in Heath. On the way the seaman told me that his brother had gone for a doctor who should be waiting for us on our return.

Within an hour we were back in the estaminet. Heath

was immediately taken upstairs and put to bed in the best
room. The doctor too, who was there already, dressed his
wound, and remained with him all night, while I slept like a
top in a loft among the potatoes and apples stored away for
the winter. My accommodation was not elaborate, but with
an old mattress, two blankets, and an old coat, it was heaven
compared with those awful nights in that horrible wood.

For three days Heath's mind wandered and the doctor
strove to save his life. This hung for a while on a very slender
thread, and during the whole of this anxious time Mme
Neusy hardly left his bedside. If she had been his own
mother, she could hardly have nursed him more devotedly.
Then the crisis passed, and he slowly began to mend. At the
end of a fortnight he was almost his old self again. By this
time, too, the hue and cry after us had died down, and we
learned that the Germans had been bluffed by kind friends.
They had spread rumours that two men, answering closely to
their description of us, had been seen making off towards
Tournai, that is to say, in the opposite direction to the
woods!

As soon as Heath was able to walk, Mme Neusy told us
that she wanted to get us both back to their own house in the
Rue Calvier. So towards the end of November we bade farewell to our friends at the estaminet and left, under cover of
night, in the company of Madame Neusy and her husband
(this was the first time that he had appeared since the first
night we spent in the woods) to return to the Rue Calvier in
easy stages. Heath could not do the whole distance in one
day. So about half-way there we put up at a cottage belonging to some friends of theirs. Everyone made a great fuss of
us. We were kissed on both cheeks by both men and women.
I did not mind this sort of thing from the ladies but I was not
keen about it on the part of two old gentlemen! We stayed
there that night and, on the following day, continued our

journey until we arrived at the house of a certain Mme Godart. She was a great friend of the Neusys. She lived in the Sentier des Bonniers on the outskirts of Wasmes.

Marie Godart was a woman of medium height and build, with a smiling face in which shone a pair of mischievous eyes. She was full of life, and appeared to be more French than Belgian, and on the night of our arrival we all sat down to the best meal we had had since our escape. We finished with cognac and coffee! Then, after the Neusys had gone—for apparently we were to stay here for a bit—we were taken upstairs to an attic which contained a small stove, two broken chairs and a double bed, the latter clean and comfortable.

Next morning we took our bearings from the only window of the room. This faced the Sentier des Bonniers but, as it was set well back in the roof, it was impossible to see much of the people passing up and down the lane. On our right was another cottage, similar to the one that we were in, and on our left we could just discern the side gate of a château surrounded by spacious grounds. Opposite, we looked out on to a blank wall, the side of a large house with its main entrance in the Rue du Dragon. There was no possible way of escape from our room other than by the stairs. We would have stood a poor chance had we been raided by the Germans.

Marie Godart had one son, Marcel, a bright, intelligent boy of eight years. He regarded Heath and myself as heroes, and did all he could to please us. At a later date, when I was in the house without Heath, he became my constant companion, and I became as fond of him as I would have of my own son. During the day we were virtually kept prisoners in our room. The reason for this was clear enough. Judging from the sound of voices that floated up the stairs from the corridor below, Marie seemed to attract a stream of visitors all day and, as few of them stayed for more than a few minutes, their presence was something of a mystery.

Punctually at nine o'clock every night the house was barred and bolted, and Heath and I invited down to the kitchen to have the meal of the day with Marie and her son. Then our hostess would unlock a cupboard, well stocked with wines and liqueurs, and invite us to take our choice and help ourselves. Soon I saw that the secret of Marie's visitors lay largely in that cupboard.

We lived at the Sentier des Bonniers for a week, and during that time the Neusys continued to supply most of our food. They also came to see us twice. On the eighth night we returned with them, again under cover of darkness, to their own home in the Rue Calvier.

6

Belgian family

We soon settled down, and in a very few days had become to all intents and purposes members of the family. Emile Neusy was a powerful, heavily built man, about forty years old, and of medium height, with a pleasant face and an abrupt hearty manner. He was optimistic to a degree; the type of man capable of making his way through life by bluff and force of personality. He did not care a damn for any German. His wife, Marie, was exactly his opposite; a frail, pale-faced little woman, with hair inclined to auburn, rather short in stature, and at least ten years his junior. Her manner was courteous, and she had already proved that she had both courage and stamina by her repeated visits to us in the wood, trudging thirteen miles every night just to bring two British soldiers food!

Both of them had been employed as commercial travellers before the war started, Emile by a miller and Marie by a firm of starch manufacturers, in Louvain. Owing to its destruction by the Germans they had now both lost their jobs. This fact did not worry Emile. He had many irons in the fire, and he worked his side lines with wonderful success.

The Neusys' one child, Robert, a boy of eleven, did not seem at all keen about us. Indeed, I am quite sure that he did not like us in the house. But this was indifference only, or possibly jealousy. There was absolutely no question as to his patriotism. Then, in addition to the family proper, there was a little maid, named Jeanne, a quaint child of about thirteen. She was not much to look at, and appeared to be simple, although subsequent events were to prove that she was far from being that indeed.

Time hung heavily on our hands, and in order to pass it Heath and I gradually took over all the housework that could be done without exposing ourselves to the view of passers-by—at the back of the house we were fairly safe as the scullery jutted out and screened us from the view of neighbours even when they were in their gardens—and, as it was really our only recreation, we did it thoroughly. In a few days their house had undergone a transformation. Everything was bright and polished, and shone like a new pin, and soon, as the result of our labours, there was really very little left for little Jeanne to do. Neusy, when he realised this, wanted to discharge her, but feeling that we were responsible for her position, and realising that if she were discharged she might talk and make things dangerous for us all, we intervened on her behalf and persuaded him to keep her on. This was wise on our part. Later I learned that one of Jeanne's sisters was fraternising with German troops stationed in the district.

A man may soldier in a battalion of eight hundred to a thousand men for many years, yet only get to know very few of them really well. He has his own small circle of friends, and is of course aware of certain men of outstanding character in the regiment, but the rest he hardly really knows at all. Were it not for their uniform he might not even recognise them at sight. And from this point of view Heath had hitherto been to me in this latter category. Although we had served in the same regiment for many years, we were only passing acquaintances until thrown together in our present strange circumstances. We now found ourselves to be very opposite in character. I always had an open mind on things. Heath had fixed opinions in favour of which he would argue, and still stick to, in spite of all the evidence adduced against them. I was a pessimist and now, of course, had much too much time in which to think and worry. This was exceedingly bad for one of my temperament. At times I became very depressed, seeing no way out of our difficulties other than by giving ourselves up to the Germans and probably being shot as spies. Heath, on the other hand, was an optimist in every sense of that word, and was always quite certain that things would work out all right and that we would get away eventually. I was of a naturally cautious cogitating disposition. Heath, on his part, completely lacked caution. He never saw danger anywhere, unless it was bang under his very nose. Indeed, this lack of it on his part brought all of us to the brink of disaster. But I must admit that his great courage saved the situation.

All I could see when I was in one of my depressions was that we were somewhere in Belgium—we did not know exactly where—cut off from all communication with the outside world and those we loved, and encircled by a ring of steel in the hands of rival combatants struggling to exterminate each other in the hatred engendered by war. In these moods, too, I would worry whether anyone in England really knew what had happened to me. I was certain that my 'knock-out' had not been seen by anyone in the battalion, whereas Heath had, no doubt, been reported as a casualty before the battalion actually retired from Wasmes. So, even if his whereabouts was at present unknown, he would only be posted as 'missing'. I was almost certainly 'presumed dead'. How was my poor wife taking it? These thoughts kept passing through my troubled mind. Captain Taylor, of the Duke of Wellington's, it is true, had promised to report my whereabouts, if he managed to get through. But I did not know at this time whether he had succeeded and, judging

rom our own experience, this now seemed exceedingly un-
ikely.

The Germans had now thoroughly organised the territory
which they had occupied both in France and Belgium.
Everything was working with machine-like precision. Ration
cards had been issued to civilians to enable them to get the
basic essentials of life, and the Neusys found it difficult at
first to provide food for us two adults because, of course, we
did not officially exist and therefore could not draw rations.
Vegetables and eggs were fairly plentiful, but meat, flour and
bread were exceedingly scarce. Neusy however did not let us
exist on short rations long. He was apparently very well
known in the district, and had many friends, bakers, butchers
and so on, whom he could trust to keep their mouths shut.
Indeed, he actually brought these friends to the house,
introduced them to us, and explained the situation. The
result was that we were soon getting all the food we wanted,
in fact far more than that to which we should have been
entitled, had we actually had ration cards!

Our bread came from an old lady, named Mme Dieu, who
lived next door. She owned two bakeries in the district, and
every morning without fail handed one of those long Belgian
loaves, about a yard in length, over the garden wall for our
consumption. She was a pious old lady, too, and never performed this kind act without crossing herself and uttering the
one word, '*Seigneur*', as the tears trickled down her wrinkled
cheeks. She was a good old soul indeed, and gave us many
things while we were her neighbours at the Neusys'.

After we had been at the Rue Calvier for about a fortnight
we had a visit from a young Belgian wine merchant named
Leon Philliperon. He could speak English quite well, and it
was a treat to be able to converse with someone in our own
tongue. He told us how the war was progressing, although
what he told us was anything but cheering. He also explained

that he belonged to an organisation that would be able to help us out of the country in due course. Before he could make any move on our behalf, however, it was absolutely essential, he said, that we should be able to speak French sufficiently well to answer any questions that might be put to us by Germans! So I began to picture myself stuck at the Rue Calvier for months! I asked how I could learn French. Philliperon replied in a very practical way. Before he left he gave us a pocket edition of Cassell's English-French and French-English dictionary. This was the most valuable thing anyone could have given two men in our peculiar position.

This dictionary changed our whole outlook on life, and we settled down to the task of learning French at once and, with its help, our very rudimentary knowledge of it increased by leaps and bounds. Napoleon is said to have maintained that an army marches on its stomach. Heath and I were not an army, but the first French words we learned from that little book were the names of things to eat and drink, and from now on we spent much of our time in these linguistic studies. We looked round at all the things in sight, and then looked up the words for them in French. After a while we even ventured on sentences! Our pronunciation must have been vile at first, and caused much merriment to our hosts, but the dictionary had soon solved our greatest difficulty: our inability to converse with the Neusys in their own tongue. In addition it gave us hope, which I had almost lost, and without which, at this time, life hardly seemed worth living.

In spite of our housework and our studies time still hung heavily on our hands. It was often difficult to think of something to fill in the gaps. One morning, however, while cleaning and tidying a bedroom cupboard, we discovered a large quantity of gaily coloured wools. Heath as usual was at once struck with a brilliant idea. He was always having bright ideas. 'Why not make some Daisy mats?' So we made a frame, and soon completed a set of Daisy mats, and presented them in due course to Madame Neusy with which to adorn her dressing-table. But they were apparently a novelty in Belgium. Instead of being used for the purpose which we had intended, her husband hawked them round to his friends as a new sideline of his. The result was that he received orders for similar ones from many quarters, and Neusy, being a keen business man, worked out their cost of production and then sold them at a handsome profit. This he handed over to us to form a fund out of which to purchase cigarettes.

One morning during my domestic duties I thought that a clock which hung high up on the wall could do with a clean, particularly as I had never seen it wound up or going since I had been in the house. I was not even certain whether it was actually in working order. So I opened the front of it and, looking inside, was dumbfounded to find a quantity of British .303 rifle ammunition tucked away neatly round its pendulum! Naturally, when Neusy returned in the evening, I told him of my discovery, and asked him why he was keeping it. Because, he said, he was also in possession of a British rifle. This he now brought out from its hiding-place, somewhere in the roof, and carried downstairs for our inspection. He was immensely proud of it as a souvenir. He had picked it up on the battlefield in the immediate vicinity of his house.

Heath was most interested—it appealed to his uncautious nature—and immediately suggested that it should be cleaned up and put in thorough working order, and always kept ready to hand, so that, in case of a raid on the house, we could 'make a fight for it' and account for a few Germans 'before they got us'. That was Heath in a nutshell: 'Fight 'em if there's a million of 'em.' He could always see only one way out, and that was usually the wrong one; the bravest perhaps,

G

but not necessarily the wisest. Neusy, a true kindred spirit, was delighted with this idea, and in his mind, I believe, pictured the fight already taking place!

With two companions of this make-up I had to do some straight and determined talking before I could make them realise the foolhardiness of this idea. If such a thing occurred, I argued, it would mean not only the death of us all, but perhaps the destruction of the whole village, even a massacre of its inhabitants! Villages had already been wiped out by the Germans for offences much less than that which they now had in mind, if the opportunity arose.

My argument cut little ice however. The rifle was cleaned daily and kept loaded, ready for instant use, if and when required. I now dreaded each successive day with that rifle in the house. Its presence preyed on my peace of mind. Again and again I insisted on its being removed, and I never let any opportunity slip without bringing up the subject. Indeed, I implored Neusy, almost on my knees, to get rid of it before it brought trouble on our heads and on those of all our friends. But this proved of no avail. So I eventually threatened to leave the house myself, and let them have their fight, if they wanted it. Marie Neusy implored me not to go, and shed a few tears. But they would not take me seriously, and finally I was compelled to deliver an ultimatum. I gave them forty-eight hours in which to make up their minds. If the rifle was still in the house after that, then I left it. And I am thankful to this day that I stuck to my guns. For, if that rifle had been found when the Germans did eventually raid the house, it would have meant the deaths of the Neusys as well as us, and perhaps that of many of their friends.

The evening after my ultimatum I was invited to spend the next day with some of the Neusys' many friends who helped to feed us. Neusy himself, of course, realised the danger of it getting too well known that he was hiding British soldiers, and did not really like us to leave his house, but he had not actually said so in the first instance, and could not now very well refuse to let us accept these invitations for fear of offending them. For us an occasional outing was a welcome change. New company and surroundings broke the inevitable monotony of our otherwise circumscribed existence.

The most extraordinary thing about these visits was that in almost every case our hosts did all they could to try to entice us to leave the Neusys, and come to live with them! They all knew the risk of harbouring us, but never seemed to see it in the light one would have expected. Naturally Heath and I refused all these invitations. We felt bound to remain under the control of Neusy as long as he was willing to keep us, or until the happy time came when we could get away. This still seemed a long way off. I asked some of these people the reason for their offers, and the replies I got were startling. One said that he was jealous of Neusy having the honour of providing for and hiding British soldiers. Another said, 'Did we not see you fight around our very homes in an attempt to stem the hated Boche? Is that not enough?' A third replied, 'We are only doing our duty as patriots in asking you to accept our hospitality.' I therefore knew that I could always find another home in the village, if I ever needed it. And now it looked as if I might!

On my return to the Rue Calvier the second evening after my ultimatum, Heath and Neusy coolly informed me that the rifle had been safely hidden away in a place where not even the Germans could ever find it. This was not good enough however. They were side-stepping the real issue, and I demanded to be shown where it was hidden. This they did not like, both being annoyed that I should doubt their word. Nevertheless, they took me up to a bedroom at the front of the house, and showed me its new hiding-place. They had taken out the window sill, removed some of the brickwork, wrapped the rifle and ammunition in waterproof paper, dropped both into the cavity, and then cemented up the wall, replaced the window sill and repapered much of the room. Or, at least, that is what they told me, and I had no good reason to doubt it. This compromise had to satisfy me, and I capitulated. I stayed on at the Neusys'. The rifle was never found by the Germans, and maybe it is still there to this day!

One evening a little later Neusy came home in high spirits. He informed us that he was taking us out to supper with some friends of his named Demoustier, who lived a few doors away. These people's son, he said, could speak good English, and on arrival the door of the house was opened by their son Maurice, who greeted us with, 'Good night! Come in' and, when at supper it fell to my lot to pass the soup and say, 'Will you have some more, Maurice?' he replied, 'If you please, sir, just a few.' So his good English did cause Heath and myself some amusement, and our French certainly made all the party roar with laughter. For they were a happy and united family: M. Demoustier and his wife, Maurice, and their daughter Gabrielle, a girl of about seventeen. After a very jolly evening we left in the early hours of the morning, Maurice bidding us, 'Good after midnight,' to which Heath replied, 'Good afternoon, Maurice! That will make a day of it!' Maurice did not see the joke. We came to know the Demoustiers still better before we left the district.

Neusy in the course of his various business activities made frequent visits to Brussels, and just before Christmas was able to secure an English newspaper which had been smuggled over the frontier from Holland. It was a copy of *The Times*, the first reliable news of the war and the outside world that we had been able to read. The price of this paper was, I believe, in the region of the equivalent of ten shillings. It was almost as good as a letter from home to us. We eagerly devoured every word on every page, even the advertisements, before—for safety of course—it was carefully destroyed in its entirety.

Neusy's affairs were clearly prospering, and he seemed to be making money fast, in consequence of which he was so generous to us that we had to be very careful what we said. It was only necessary to remark that we should like so-and-so, and off he would go to Brussels to get it, regardless of the cost; and when one remembers that the distance from Wasmes to Brussels is approximately thirty-five miles, and that this meant a night away from home, it underlines his generosity. He seemed always to want to satisfy our every whim. Nothing was ever too much trouble where we were concerned. I remember, for example, remarking one day that I really would like a good cup of tea for a change. So next morning, without informing us of his intentions, he was *en route* for Brussels to get it, and returned the following evening with two pounds of the finest China tea! Heaven knows what he must have paid for it!

Sometimes we tried our hands at cooking the family dinner, and on these occasions did our best to make it entirely English in character. The Neusys seemed to enjoy this change from their ordinary diet almost as much as we did. Some of their tastes were certainly odd, and we had difficulty in subscribing to them. Belgians seem very fond of raw food, especially cured fish, and Neusy would eat bloaters and cured haddock with evident relish, just as they came from the fishmonger! I struggled manfully but could never acquire this taste.

One afternoon Marie Neusy was visited by a man and woman who were evidently of a superior station in life and asked point blank to see the two British soldiers hidden in the house. Marie was surprised and very cautious, thinking that they might be Germans. Even when they said they were the Princess Marie de Croy and Prince Réginald from Château Bellignies, and that they represented an organisation which could help to get us out of the country, she still denied all knowledge of our existence. It was only later that we learnt that they really were the Prince and Princess. Their visit had been a genuine attempt to help us.[1]

On Christmas Eve we were invited to another party at the Demoustiers'; a farewell one to Maurice. He had obtained permission from the Germans to go to Holland as a student to complete his studies in chemistry, when as a matter of fact he was going to England to join the Belgian Army! The 'student' stunt was an excuse by which many young Belgians managed to leave occupied territory. This party was a great success. There was plenty to eat and drink, and music to which to listen, and finished with *La Brabançonne* (the Belgian national anthem) followed by 'God Save the King'. Maurice promised to let his parents know of his safe arrival in England by inserting a notice in the Press on a certain date. I cannot remember the name of the paper, but it was one that published some of its news in French for the benefit of Belgian refugees. So, in due course, Neusy journeyed to Brussels and returned with the issue of the specified date. In it, sure enough, was an insertion that, when translated, ran something like this:

Have arrived Folkestone. Now going to London and then to the Front. Maurice.

Here in fact was a method of communication with the outside world via Holland about which the Germans knew little yet. The risk of smuggling in newspapers across the

1. If Marie Neusy had trusted the de Croys, Beaumont and Heath might well have got out of the country much sooner. This episode illustrates one of the main difficulties with which the organisation had to contend, namely, knowing whom they could trust, on the one hand, and getting other people, even those who they were trying to help, to trust them, on the other.   *Editor*

frontier was, however, great, and their price almost pro-
hibitive in consequence.

After I got home Maurice often used to write to me from
the Front. Here is one of his letters, dated July 29th, 1916:

My dear,

    *I am on the front in the Trenches and near the English Soldiers.
English Soldiers are coming each day in our camp, and they are giving
to the Belgians several things, knives, jams, corned beef and marma-
lades. They are all good friends for us, I have a gigantic Knife and
am very contented of it.*

    *Are you already in good health, and what do you know with the
end of the War. The English Soldiers near the Belgians, these are
very courageous, their bombardments are terribles, give me news.*

Your Friend

Maurice

Sergeant B.215

Christmas Day itself we spent quietly at the Rue Calvier.
Mme Dieu, the good old lady who lived next door, gave us a
large bottle of wine for this occasion. It must have been of
some rare vintage and lay in a wine basket. This no doubt
enhanced its quality. I cannot claim to be a connoisseur in
wine although I could at least tell that this was a good
vintage.

As a precaution we made plans against a possible German
raid. We dug a hole in the cellar deep enough to take us both
in a sitting position, and made a wooden lid for it. The idea
was that we should get into it, and then the Neusys would
put on the lid, and cover that with coke. The spot would
then look like an ordinary heap of coke provided the
Germans gave us sufficient warning of their coming. Another
possible hiding-place was the tank which collected rain water
from the roof to supply the house. This could be entered by a

flap in the floor of one of the rooms, normally hidden by a mat, and to make getting in easy we constructed a short ladder. This we fitted inside it. We never actually tried either of these hiding-places and, I think, had we been forced to use either of them, we should have soon been suffocated. Both were practically air-tight! If the house was not actually surrounded, we planned to escape through the landing window at the top of the stairs. It was an easy drop from that on to the roof of the scullery below, and down again to the garden. Then we would be able to climb over the wall at the back, and reach the fields.

7

Suspected

B Y THE end of 1914 the Germans had come to learn that
a number of British soldiers were still at large in occupied
territory hidden by civilians. So they issued a warning
through local authorities, and also posted notices, to the
effect that any soldiers of the Allies, who were still at large,
were to report to the police immediately. They would then
be treated as prisoners of war. But if they failed to do so
before January 15th they would be shot as spies, whether in
uniform or not. At the same time the civil population were
warned that the penalty for harbouring a British soldier was
death. I never actually saw this notice myself, but I had no
doubt about it. It was freely discussed by the Neusys and
their friends. They did not seem the least disturbed by it
however. In fact they went on just the same! The idea of
giving us up, to save their skins, never seemed to enter their
heads!

As few, if any, of these men had surrendered themselves by
January 15th, the Governor General now issued another
order. This instructed the Belgian police to make an immediate house-to-house search for fugitives, and to render a
report to regional commandants to the effect that their
respective towns and villages were clear of them. Again the
Germans, after giving an order, had placed the onus of
executing it on the local authorities. This was in our favour.
The Belgians were lazy, either by nature or intent, and in

most cases rendered their report without having taken much trouble to find out. Nevertheless, the appearance of any Germans in the Rue Calvier now caused some anxiety in our house. But they invariably turned out to be men looking for girls, and not soldiers or police looking for fugitives.

During the long weary winter evenings which followed Christmas it was often difficult to know what to do with ourselves in order to pass the time. Domestic chores and learning the lingo were hardly enough to keep us always occupied. Sometimes the Neusys would sing to us in French, and we would return the compliment by singing to them in English, and after a while, having heard their French songs over and over again, Heath and I were able to sing them to the Neusys, although we never understood what half the words meant. The Neusys never seemed to be able to grasp the words of our English songs. M. Neusy was also a good actor, and loved to entertain us by mimicking various people he had seen on the stage in Brussels. He was also very fond of going over and acting the events of our arrival at his house on the morning of our escape from the hospital. This scene he aptly named 'Reconstruction'.

When the night was still, I would often wander out into the garden to listen to the deep booming of the guns on the Western Front. How one wondered what was happening! Sometimes their sound seemed nearer. This raised our hope that the British would soon come through the village again and liberate us all from our predicament. At others those guns seemed further away than ever but we soon realised that our hopes were either being raised or lowered merely by the direction of the wind!

Heath was still suffering from the effects of his exposure in the woods. He was repeatedly catching chills, which often brought on bronchitis, and when this happened, it meant calling in the doctor. He usually prescribed hot red wine!

This, and a few days in bed, seemed to restore him to his usual health. One evening, when we were chatting and talking about wine, the subject of beer cropped up, and I happened to mention that I had almost forgotten the taste of it! Next day a huge cask was mysteriously delivered to the house, presumably on Neusy's instructions. He invited us to help ourselves as often as we liked! It really was unsafe to make a remark of this kind or express any wish in his hearing because, if it were at all possible, he would gratify it, regardless of the cost to himself in money, time or trouble.

Neusy's schemes for making money prospered, and as a result of them a fair sum soon accumulated in the house. Further, for some strange reason best known to himself, he made Heath keeper of the family purse, his treasure chest and safe being a tin box which he hid somewhere by day and kept under his pillow at night. Heath now paid the bills, and gave Marie Neusy the cash for incidental and household expenses. He was often reproved by Neusy for being too generous in this respect.

Meanwhile we were progressing steadily with our French. In fact we progressed so fast that we often got into trouble for saying too much or saying the wrong thing. I well remember one incident which caused a spot of bother at the family table. Robert, Neusy's son, was a bit of a wild spark, and often used words to Jeanne, the maid, which we did not understand and could not find in our dictionary. On this particular occasion Heath and Jeanne were engaged in a bit of repartee, and Heath called her by a name which we had often heard Robert use to the girl when his parents were absent. No sooner was this word out of Heath's mouth than Neusy was on his feet demanding to know who had taught him to use it. Heath, not wishing to give the boy away, said that he had heard it while he was in hospital, but honestly did not know what it meant. Neusy refused to accept this apology. He told Heath bluntly that he did not believe him, and it took me a long time to calm him down again.

One evening Neusy returned from Brussels well pleased with himself. While eating his dinner he kept chuckling audibly and, on my asking the cause of his merriment, he told us what he at least had thought the greatest fun. When he left the tram at Mons, he was stopped, he said, by a German official who demanded to see his identity card, and also felt round his pockets for the *verboten* newspaper. Now in the breast pocket of Neusy's coat was, as a matter of fact, a copy of *The Times* and, as the German felt it, he exclaimed:

'*Ah, papier!*'

But Neusy was ready for him.

'*Non, non, cigares,*' he replied, and, drawing out a fat one, handed it to the German.

Then, before the official had recovered from his astonishment, Neusy bade him good night and hurried off. This incident he seemed to look on as a huge joke in spite of the very serious consequences that it so well might have had.

Of all the many people we met while at the Rue Calvier one only seemed at all antagonistic towards us. This was a Belgian, named Geoffrey Litard, a merchant from the town of Quevacamps, a tall thin man with something wrong with his eyes. This gave him a peculiarly evil appearance. Heath and I, for some reason, nicknamed him Giffy, and by their actions and conversation when together I surmised that Giffy and Marie Neusy had been on friendly terms in the days before the war. Certainly there was no doubt that our presence in the house rather queered his pitch, and perhaps prevented him from making more of it. He did not for some reason seem to mind me, but he hated the very sight of Heath, and openly showed his dislike of him. I could foresee trouble brewing between these two, and was certain that, sooner or later, it would end in a real row.

This came about sooner than I had expected, and on an afternoon when I happened to be out of the house. Heath was upstairs, and Giffy arrived, exclaiming to Marie, 'Where's that —————, Arthur?' Unfortunately Heath heard, and answered him appropriately from the top of the stairs. Giffy, in a rage, rushed up them, just as Heath started to dash down them and, when they collided, Giffy got the worst of the encounter. He left the house, nursing a badly bruised face and vowing eternal vengeance on that —————— Heath. He was a dangerous man to have upset. Indeed, I wondered at the time whether it was Giffy who put the German secret police on our tracks a few weeks later.

It was now about the second week in February and all seemed quiet on our front. Heath and I had now managed to evade being caught for over four months, and this had, I suppose, lulled us into a false sense of security. A visit from the Mayor of Wasmes now suddenly startled us out of it however. Or, I should say, startled me out of mine. Heath's optimism prevented him anticipating any kind of danger. He, the Mayor, it now appeared, had overheard two women, both known to be prostitutes who fraternised with German soldiers, gossiping in a café, in the course of which they said that Marie Neusy was hiding English soldiers in her house. So the Mayor, who had known Marie since she was a child, now wanted to know if that was really true. Marie could hardly deny it.

'Well, Marie,' he said, 'if I always did what these Germans tell me, I should hand them over to German headquarters, but, being a Belgian and a patriot, I cannot bring myself to do that. As I am unfortunately responsible to the German authorities however, and have reported that Wasmes has been carefully searched and found clear of fugitives, I am afraid they simply must go. They must leave *this* village. But where they go, my dear, is no concern of mine!'

He also pointed out to Marie that it was just as easy for the Germans to learn of our whereabouts as it had been for him to do so himself. Whereupon, terribly upset at this unexpected turn of events, Marie promised that she would do as he wished. We would leave, she said, that night.

When Neusy himself returned we discussed the situation, but he did not seem much concerned and treated the Mayor's visit with his customary indifference. As for Heath, he maintained that the Mayor's visit was 'all bunk'. He was going to stay on 'even if all the prostitutes in the whole of Belgium knew where he was'. I treated the matter seriously. The Mayor's warning must be heeded, I said, and in saying that I was not only thinking of saving my own skin. I was also thinking of the danger in which we placed all those generous people who had already risked so much to befriend us. Heated argument ensued, and Heath as usual was adamant. He simply could not see that he was risking the Neusys' lives; that it was not fair, indeed not right, to sponge on their generous hospitality any longer. I just could not convince him and, in the end, I decided to leave by myself. I had plenty of friends, I knew, within a radius of two miles who would welcome me with open arms.

On hearing my decision Neusy accepted it reluctantly, and asked where I would like to go. 'I leave that to you,' I replied. 'Take me where you think best.' So, after a little pondering, he decided that he would take me to Marie Godart at the Sentier des Bonniers. She could be trusted not to talk, he said, and that was all that mattered.

Back to the attic and solitude, separated from the Neusy family, deprived of Heath's cheery optimism, I now soon began to get depressed. I seemed to lose all hope, and my mind was beset by horrible imaginings. I began to worry

bout my wife, and my four brothers who must now all be in
he war. What was happening to them? Were they still alive?

began to suffer from insomnia too, and when I did fall
sleep I was troubled by dreams in which I found myself in
German hands. More than once I dreamt that I was up
against a wall, facing a firing party, and woke up soaked in
perspiration.

During the day I spent most of my time watching the
street and the château that stood on the left of Marie's house.
Something mysterious was going on there, I was quite sure,
and it became for me a welcome centre of interest. At least
it provided something to think about and, as the days passed,
the mystery deepened. On several occasions I saw a young
man, accompanied either by a woman or a child, walk down
the street and, after cautiously looking round in all directions,
clearly to see whether their movements were being watched,
hurry through the side gate and disappear into the house.
Then, a little later, the woman or the child, whichever it had
been, would come out, and leave alone, without any of the
caution that was so obvious when they entered it. There was
something very secret in connection with this château.

I told Marie Godart about this, but apart from the fact
that it belonged to a wealthy family who were out of the
country, and that it was being looked after by a caretaker,
she could give me no information or throw any light on the
mystery.

For three days I was confined to Marie Godart's attic.
During this period I only saw Marie herself at night, when I
was invited down to the kitchen after the house had been
locked up. My only visitor during the day was Marie's son,
Marcel. He brought me my food, and kept me alive with his
boyish talk. He looked upon me as a hero. We hit it off
together well and, as I had left the dictionary at the Rue
Calvier with Heath, he became my tutor in French. My

lessons were mainly taken from old newspapers and, as he could not speak English, these were chiefly on pronunciation. How the boy would laugh when I got stuck with a real tongue-twister! But he would never let me rest until I had it right. Then he would go out scouting in the village, to see what the Germans were up to, and on his return faithfully report to me the result of his reconnaissance. Young though he was, this boy was a true patriot. He hated Germans with all his might.

Marcel was also constantly begging money from his mother, and kept raiding his money-box to buy cigarette tobacco in the village. For, although he was only eight years old, he smoked heavily, and the only tobacco he could obtain was strong black Belgian shag. This was rank to the taste, but he could not get anything else, and we would smoke cigarette after cigarette together as we sat beside the tiny stove that warmed my attic. My chief trouble was that I had nothing to occupy my time or mind while Marcel was out scouting, but on the third or fourth morning of my stay at Marie Godart's I was searching my waistcoat in the hope of finding a little tobacco dust with which to make a cigarette, when I felt something hard in the lining which turned out to be a bit of lead pencil. This gave me an idea. I would try to draw! I had no paper, it is true, but the walls of my attic were whitewashed, and I had plenty of scope on them. So I commenced. I had never been keen on drawing at school, and my first efforts were laughable, but as I persevered my pictures slowly began to resemble the objects which I was trying to depict—at least to some extent. My chief subjects in my present state of mind were naturally Germans; Germans with and without helmets, and Germans of all sorts, shapes and sizes; and also, in my lighter moments, trees, flowers and birds. These drawings much amused the boy. His mother did not quite approve of this new style of decoration which was transforming her room into a sort of art gallery, but she allowed me to go on, and this pastime prevented me from thinking too much of other things. I felt much better for it.

After several whole days in the attic Marie Godart suggested that I should take my place as one of the family, and go down to the kitchen during the day. This, she did admit, had its dangers, and people who came to the house might talk. If I did not speak, however, no one would suspect who I was, and she would introduce me, she said, as one of her relations who was unfortunately deaf and dumb. Naturally I was glad of a chance to escape from the solitude and dismal surroundings of my attic, and as I was pretty good at acting, the role of being deaf and dumb appealed to me. Little did I realise the odd situations in which I should get landed, and the part proved much more difficult to play than I had anticipated.

Marie had many visitors, which occasionally included German officers and soldiers, and it was not long before I found out many things that had kept me guessing hitherto. Marie had no husband. At least, I had never seen him about the house. Neither had I ever heard anyone refer to him, and I had already questioned Marcel as to whether his father was away at the war or whether he was dead. He answered 'No' to each question, and volunteered no further information, and I was reluctant to enquire into the matter. There might be some family skeleton hidden in a cupboard! After all, it was no business of mine.

Naturally, too, I had often wondered how Marie made her living, and now soon tumbled to the fact that her income was derived from two sources, namely, drink and immorality. She sold wines and liquors which had been smuggled over the French frontier at high prices to all who had the money to buy them. That I knew already. Now I found that she also kept what we would call in our country a disorderly house, letting her rooms to all comers, whether

H

officers or men, Germans or Belgians, who brought women with them. Those who came in merely for a drink, or to buy a bottle of brandy or wine, came straight through to the kitchen, where the deaf-and-dumb relation soon became a centre of interest and sympathy. Many visitors stood me drinks! The other class of visitor I often heard but very rarely saw. Marie ushered them into the bedrooms, and made sure that they never strayed into the kitchen.

When I first discovered that this was going on in the house I had serious thoughts of moving to more select quarters. On reflection I comforted myself however with the thought that I was not there through any fault of my own, and decided that it would be wiser to stay where I was. In the light of subsequent events I am truly thankful that I did. Meanwhile, as Marie's contraband continued to arrive (at night, of course), I got to know many of the smugglers who supplied her.[1]

One morning a customer came to Marie's house to buy a bottle of wine and, when she introduced her deaf-and-dumb relation to him, he was tickled to death. It was the post-master of Wasmes, one of Neusy's friends, who had met me many times before at the Rue Calvier. We all enjoyed the joke on Marie, and he was very pleased to see me again, and before he left, invited me to his house and gave me directions as to how to reach it. So next morning, taking him at his word, I set off to get there in disguise. I carried a carpenter's bag on my back with a saw and a plane sticking out of either end. This seemed an excellent disguise. No one took the least notice of me, as I threaded my way through the streets, and M. Ruchard and his wife and daughter were delighted to see me. I passed a most enjoyable day in their company. His

---

1. Several years later I spent a night with the whole gang at their headquarters in a cottage near the woods on the French frontier close to Maubeuge.   *Author*

daughter could speak a little English, and we spent much of the time teaching one another our own languages.

The postmaster himself told me something of Marie Godart's history. She had seen better days, he said, and at one time kept a large house with a staff of three servants, but her husband had turned out to be a rotter. He ran through all her money, and deserted her just before the war started. Knowing Marie's occupation I remarked that perhaps she deserved to be treated like that. I had put my foot right in it! He demanded to know what I meant, and in order to justify myself I told him all that I had discovered about Marie. Whereupon he merely laughed, and pointed out that the moral code in Belgium was not so strict as ours in England. There were several similar houses in the village, he said, and proceeded to tell me off for speaking ill of Marie while I was being sheltered by her. She was a good woman really, well known and much loved in the village, and always ready to give her last penny to anyone in distress. I could not possibly have fallen, he said, into better hands.

He also showed me a bag of letters which had been posted by British soldiers as they passed through the village during the retreat, and which he had been unable to despatch. The Germans had arrived too quickly. Some of the envelopes had the name and regiment of the writer on the back, and I recognised many of them at once as belonging to my own unit. He assured me that they would be sent off on the very day the war ended.

When I returned to the Sentier des Bonniers I felt much happier, and the visit to the postmaster was followed by many others. These helped me to make progress with my French. His daughter was an able tutor. The postmaster and I also became firm friends, and he and his family did all in their power to make my lot happier.

One morning a few weeks later I was busy in Marie's

kitchen preparing the vegetables for the eternal *soupe legume* when I heard heavy footsteps in the corridor and, as the door opened, I glanced up and got a shock which made my heart jump into my throat. In the doorway stood the biggest German I had ever seen! He enquired for Marie but, remembering my role of deaf mute, I just looked daft and made no articulate reply. Luckily at this moment Marie herself came in from the garden, and greeted him heartily, gave me a reassuring glance, and introduced me to him as her 'afflicted relative'. He proved to be an old friend of Marie, a German she had known before the war. He had been on the Western Front, and Marie managed to extract some of the latest war news from him. This, coming from a German, was very interesting. He seemed far from happy as to the way in which things were going, and spoke sadly of many of his friends being '*kaput*'. Before he left he stood Marie and her 'afflicted relative' a drink. We clinked glasses in true continental style.

The cottage next door was used by an old man as a workshop. Marie seemed to be afraid of him. She was continually warning me that he was dangerous, and implored me never to let him see me either in the house or garden, but I was never able to discover the reason for this, and she herself introduced me to him later on. Perhaps she had been misinformed and had been misjudging him. Anyhow this change of front enabled me to spend many an interesting hour helping him with the things he was trying to make. His company, and working with him, sometimes led me to forget the bloody Germans.

Twice a week Marie engaged a charwoman to give a hand with the washing and housework. She was a very talkative old lady, and I had to watch my role very carefully. It may have been by design, because she suspected me—although I think it was only by accident—but she always contrived to sit next to me at meals, and often addressed her conversation to me until, realising that this was useless, she would beg my pardon and excuse herself, saying she had forgotten. These lapses on her part seemed to amuse Marie for some reason. She never dared look at me for fear that she would burst out laughing and give the show away.

Although things were quiet, I could not really forget the Germans. They kept me awake at night and in a funk by day, the former particularly as a patrol had, out of all the other places they might so easily have chosen, selected the corner of the street just under my window as the spot to while away two or three hours every night, chatting and smoking while off duty. The clatter of the butts of their rifles on the cobble-stones, the tread of their heavily shod feet, and their guttural voices kept me awake for hours on end. And if they did not do this, the repeated short, sharp reports of a rifle, fired by a sentry at the Belgians who went every night to a coal-dump nearby to scrounge what they considered to be their own property, did the same thing almost as effectively.

On two occasions Zeppelins passed directly over our heads, creating a terrible din, on their way to deal death and destruction to the helpless and innocent at home, and within forty-eight hours we would read the results of their expeditions in the local newspapers, usually to the effect that half of London had been destroyed. And we did not know how much to believe.

One evening Marcel came in with the bad news that the Germans had been raiding all the big houses in Pâturages. This village was not very far away, and this information was certainly rather disturbing. So I sent him round to the Rue Calvier to advise Heath to shift his quarters and move else-where, if he valued his life. But he remained obdurate. He merely sent a message back to tell me 'not to get the wind up'.

Next morning at daybreak I heard great activity in the street below my window. Orders were being shouted, and Germans rushing hither and thither. For one ghastly moment I thought they had come for me at last. They were only raiding the château at the corner however, and, as I listened, I heard Marie at her door engaged in repartee with some of the searchers, many of whom were well known to her as the result of her business. Most of it was, I am much afraid, wasted on them. Germans have little sense of humour. Before the raiders left she was brazen enough to ask the officer in command when he was going to search her house. 'Never,' he replied, 'I should be wasting my time.' On hearing this I felt that I ought to feel safe and secure at the Sentier des Bonniers. But I had a horrid feeling that something awful was destined to happen very soon.

8

Police raid

I HAD just sat down one day at noon to a piece of steak, sent along by Mme Ruchard, the postmaster's wife, when Gabrielle Demoustier burst in, crying bitterly. The Germans had raided Neusy's house, and had arrested Marie and Heath! I had long expected this. But when the news did come, it was a terrible shock, and, after Gabrielle had departed, I felt that I could not really stay at the Sentier des Bonniers safely with Marie Godart any longer. It was too near the Rue Calvier. Every minute I expected the Germans to arrive and arrest me. I was anxious, too, not to endanger Marie and her boy by my presence any longer. Clearly it would be wise to get far away from the district. But where was I to go?

Marie and I spent the rest of the day on tenterhooks, listening for the slightest sound that would herald the arrival of the Germans. By evening we were both a bundle of nerves, the slightest sound from the street making us start like hunted hares. Indeed, Marcel seemed the only one capable of thinking, and now proposed that he should take me to his grandmother (Marie's mother) who lived in a village about four miles away. I jumped at this suggestion, and in a few minutes was on my way to La Bouverie where the old lady lived.

It was an adventure for the boy being abroad during hours prohibited by the Germans, and he chuckled with glee as we trudged along, and then dodged behind a house, or a clump of bushes, to let a German patrol pass by. At length, about an hour later, we arrived at Grandma Godart's without having been challenged. She was a delightful old lady, wonderfully active for her years which, she informed me, numbered eighty. But that night I could not go to sleep. My heart was heavy, thinking of the fate of my old comrade Heath and poor, brave Marie Neusy. How long, too, would it be before they got me. I wondered?

Eventually I must have dozed off for I was woken up in the early hours by a terrific banging at the street door. The Germans had come for me at last! That is what I thought at once. I leapt out of bed, slipped on my trousers, and with my boots in my hand, and the remainder of my clothing festooned round my neck, prepared to do a get-away as best I could. Cautiously I opened the window and looked out. No Germans were to be seen at the back of the house. It was a ten-foot drop to the lawn below, and I had one leg already over the window sill, when Marcel rushed into my room, shouting that Heath and Emile Neusy had arrived! At first I could scarcely believe it. Then, as Grandma Godart let them in, I heard Heath asking for me. I dashed down, and at first I could only stare at him in blank amazement, a Heath who had lost that happy cocksure manner, and looked a tired, haunted, hunted man. Only gradually did he recover sufficiently to tell me the extraordinary story of how he managed to escape.

At about nine o'clock that fateful morning, i.e. the morning before, three rings on the bell at the back gate had signalled the arrival of friends at the Neusy establishment, and Marie, who was engaged in some household chore in the kitchen, did not even trouble to see who it was, as visitors of that kind walked in without ceremony. But, as the kitchen door opened, Marie looked up, and her customary greeting froze on her lips. She suddenly found herself confronted, not by friends, but by two strange men, both covering her with pistols!

These men now informed her that they were members of the German secret police, and demanded to know the whereabouts of the two English soldiers she was hiding in her house. Poor Marie was properly trapped, and knew it. But she never lost her head. Heath was still in bed in the room above the kitchen and, in order to give him a chance to get away, she strenuously denied any knowledge of two English soldiers in as loud a voice as she could, hoping that Heath was awake and would hear her.

Heath was awake and did hear her. Quietly slipping out of bed, he listened at the top of the stairs and, fortunately for him, now knew enough French to understand the Germans' bullying questions and Marie's answers, more or less. He quickly realised that he was in a very tight corner, particularly as the Germans, without further parley with Marie, now decided to search the house. So, while one remained with her, to see that she gave no alarm, the other commenced the search, and for some unknown and lucky reason elected to begin with the cellar. He started to descend the cellar stairs. This gave Heath time to think. At first he thought of cracking the German on the head with a quart bottle of ammonia, which he happened to have up there, when he entered his room, but quickly gave up this idea. He guessed they would be armed, and being two to one he would not really have a chance. But now there was no time to lose. He could hear heavy footsteps climbing the cellar stairs. So, quickly deciding on flight, and in no other clothing than a long white night shirt, belonging to Neusy, and a pair of his own socks, he slipped out of the landing window, the way of escape that had been planned beforehand and the only one offering itself at the moment. From this it was only a drop of a few feet on to the roof of the scullery. But this way of escape, like the hiding-places we had planned, had never actually been tested. The unforeseen happened. When Heath dropped on to the roof, one of his legs went bang through the slates!

The sound of the crash brought matters to a head. The German who was with Marie rushed to the scullery door. So did Marie and, as she arrived there first, she locked it and attempted to throw the key into the fire. The German, seeing her intention, floored her with a terrific blow from his fist and, recovering the key, quickly unlocked the door, and rushed out at exactly the same moment as Heath was about to jump from the roof, and seeing the German below him, jumped straight on to his neck. It was the only thing for him to do. The German had a pistol! And the German, being corpulent, would be bound to break his fall.

Heath, having the advantage of being on top, was the first up, and dashed for the wall at the bottom of the garden, but had not covered many yards before the German, who had struggled up to a sitting position, started firing at him with his automatic pistol. At the first shot Heath swerved, and then started to zig-zag. So, although the German fired five shots, not one found its mark before Heath reached the wall. This was seven feet high and topped with pieces of glass embedded in the cement, to keep out marauders. Heath leapt at it twice, but failed to get a hold. By this time the German, having regained his feet, was running after him down the garden in pursuit. Heath, hearing him coming, did not wait to be caught. He jumped over the low dividing wall into Mme Dieu's garden next door, and started to run again, but tripped up and measured his length in a cabbage patch. So, by the time he had picked himself up, the German had him covered from the other side of the wall, and in perfect English ordered him to put up his hands.

Heath was brought to bay but not beat. He took no notice of the order to put up his hands, merely looked soft, and replied in French to the effect that he did not understand. Again he was ordered to put up his hands, this time in French, and, of course, this time up they went. By now, however, the other German had reached the landing window, and, seeing the situation, commenced shouting instructions to his junior in the garden. This was a false move on his part. For, according to German etiquette, no German may answer his superior with his back turned to him. So, as this one turned about to reply, Heath seized his opportunity. He made a dash for and a frantic leap at the wall at the bottom of Mme Dieu's garden, and this time gained a hold, and a warning shout from the German at the window came too late for the German in the garden. He turned round just in time to see Heath's leg disappear over the wall as he dived into the field the other side, and to have one more shot. But that was too late, too! Again he missed! Heath had escaped for the time being by a route that neither of his pursuers could follow without a ladder, and this was not available, with which to get over the wall. Their only alternative now was to go round from one or other end of the Rue Calvier in the hope of cutting him off. But, as both Germans were on the corpulent side, they did not try, and the German in the garden returned to the house to get a severe 'strafing' from his superior for failing to get his man. Meanwhile Heath was careering cross country in Neusy's nightshirt, with another lease of his life in his hands, thanks entirely to German etiquette.

While the two Germans were arguing over his escape, Marie Neusy picked herself up and sat down in the scullery in a dazed state, taking little interest in the proceedings. The blow which she had received had robbed her temporarily of her senses, but, as soon as she had recovered sufficiently to realise what had happened, the Germans started interrogating her and now questioned her for nearly an hour. They maintained that the man who had escaped was an English soldier. But Marie was not to be trapped into admitting that and strenuously denied it. The man who had escaped was a Belgian friend of hers, she said, who had been frightened away by their untimely visit and threatening attitude. And when she was asked what a man friend was doing in bed in her house while her husband was away, she refused to answer, hoping that her silence would lead them to think that she wished to keep this from her husband, and thereby disabuse their minds of the runaway being an Englishman.

The senior German police officer now arrested Marie and, leaving his colleague behind to hold any person who turned up during the day, walked her off, forbidding her to speak to anyone on the way, unless he gave her permission. Unfortunately for him he had left his car some distance away from the house, in case the noise of it had warned the Neusys of his coming, and if he thought he could stop Marie talking by merely telling her not to he was sadly mistaken. She broadcast the fact that he was a German policeman, and had arrested her for nothing, to everyone they met at the top of her voice, and this disregard for authority made him furious, with the result that she was hurried along at speed with scant ceremony and, when they did reach the car, literally bundled into it. Then the policeman set off for Mons. There Marie was put in prison.

The news of Marie's arrest spread rapidly through the village. So the German left behind in the house had a rough time at the hands of a continuous stream of sympathisers who called to find what it was all about, or to protest against it. It was fortunate that she had happened to be the only one of the family at home that morning. Emile was away at Brussels on one of his foraging expeditions. Robert had gone to spend a few days with relatives. Jeanne had been sent on an errand, and was not due back until late in the afternoon.

So their friends had ample opportunity to warn all three of the raid before they returned to the house to find themselves being questioned by the Germans.

Jeanne was the first to get back. She was accompanied by Emile Neusy's sister who, on hearing of the raid and Marie's arrest, had intercepted her, and now returned with her to get the facts first-hand. In this she was unsuccessful. The policeman who had been left behind had become thoroughly rattled by this time by the questions fired and the insults thrown at him by numerous callers, and had no patience for any of Marie's relatives. On learning that she did not belong to the household, he ordered her off the premises.

He now turned his attention to Jeanne, and seeing that she was not much more than a child naturally thought that he had an easy task in extracting from her all the information he required to condemn Marie Neusy. In this he made a profound mistake. Jeanne showed pluck and intelligence far beyond her years. In spite of her tender age, and being questioned at the point of the pistol, she was not afraid, and treated the threatening attitude of the German policeman as a joke. She told him to put away his 'fifty-centime pistol' (meaning that it was a toy). Only then, she said, would she answer his questions, and thinking that he was going to get something in the way of evidence out of her, the man did as he was bid. Then he asked how many English soldiers her mistress had hidden in the house. She answered 'None'. She denied that she had ever seen any soldiers there during her service with the Neusys.

'But,' said the German, 'what about the Englishman who was in the house when you left this morning?'

Jeanne already knew that Heath had got away, and was not to be trapped so easily. She replied that there was never an Englishman in the house, but that there had been a Belgian who was Mme Neusy's lover. This man often came to the house, she said, when M. Neusy was away on business. This was a marvellous coincidence. Jeanne, without any collusion with Marie, deliberately raised the same doubt about the man who had escaped really being a British soldier in this man's mind, as her mistress had raised in the other's mind in answer to the questions asked her only a few hours before!

Later in the evening this other policeman returned with a squad of German soldiers, and every house in the Rue Calvier was turned upside down. They found a few articles in Neusy's house which were to some extent incriminating. Under the eaves they discovered several German bayonets and other souvenirs that Neusy had picked up on the battle-field. On top of a high cupboard they found a copy of a supplement to *The Times* of December 19th, containing copies of all the papers and notes between the nations leading up to the declaration of war and fixing the blame for it firmly on Germany. I well remember reading that supplement when Neusy brought it home, but how it came to be where it was discovered, or who put it there, remains a mystery. Heath and I had always been particularly careful to destroy all English newspapers by burning them immediately after we had finished reading them. Anyhow, it was the only English thing they did find, although they were to make the most of it as evidence at the trial.

They also discovered quantities of rationed foodstuffs in which Neusy had no right to be trading. So they confiscated his money, seven hundred francs that Heath had left behind in his room in his hurried flight. But they never found that British rifle and ammunition which had been such a bone of contention between us. This, to the best of my knowledge and belief, still lies in the wall where it was hidden. They searched Mme Dieu's house next door, too, and as the policeman lifted up the valance which hung round her bed

e suddenly saw something move. His nerves were on edge.
Taking no chances, he fired point blank. But it was only a
cat which had selected that spot to bring up a family of
kittens! Luckily for pussy he missed. He must have been a
rotten shot, that policeman! Then they both sat down to
wait for Neusy to return but, as he did not turn up, they
soon got tired, and, telling Jeanne to inform him that, if he
liked to come to Mons next day, he could see his wife and
have his money back, they departed, leaving the house
unguarded.

Meanwhile Heath had made a clean get-away. As he
negotiated the wall at the bottom of Mme Dieu's garden,
he gashed the inside of his leg on the broken glass that sur-
mounted it. A few cuts did not deter him however, and
landing in a ploughed field on the other side, he dashed
across it until he came to a narrow lane down which he
turned until he came to a forge. Two Belgians were working
there. Seeing an open passage right through it, he darted
through, both Belgians dropping their tools in amazement as
the ghostly apparition flashed past. On the grass at the back
of the forge two women were spreading their washing out to
dry in the sun, according to Belgian custom. Catching sight
of a dishevelled, wild-eyed man, clad in nothing but a night
shirt and socks, with blood streaming down his legs, they
gave one scream and took to their heels. Things like this did
not deflect Heath's course, however, and he ran on until he
came to some gardens at the back of a few cottages. Here,
noticing that the door of one of them was slightly ajar, he
jumped the low fence, and in a few more strides was inside.
The room was empty, and he sank exhausted into a chair by
the fire, observing from the tub that stood on the floor that
it must be washing day. So—although to this day he cannot
say why he did it—he dragged off his muddy socks, or rather
what was left of them, and flung them into the washtub!

A few minutes later the lady of the house, coming downstairs, got the shock of her life. She found a strange, wild-eyed, bloodstained man sitting at her fireside in his night attire, and Heath was now forced to struggle to explain himself. He also apologised deeply for trespassing, and humbly craved shelter for the time being. He had struck lucky! She was a true patriot, soon made him comfortable, and even provided him with some of her husband's own clothes. Before long, too, she had fetched a doctor to attend to his cuts, which were still bleeding freely, and this proved to be the same one as had attended him at the Rue Calvier. Further, he had already heard about the raid and Madame Neusy's arrest, and advised Heath to remain where he was, while he went to Mons himself to meet Neusy on his return from Brussels and tell him of Heath's whereabouts. As a matter of fact at least a dozen people went to Mons to meet Neusy that night, but only the doctor knew where Heath had anchored down, and he was far too wise to tell anyone but Neusy himself about that.

On hearing what had happened while he was away from home Neusy decided to go direct to the cottage to see Heath, instead of returning to his own house in the Rue Calvier. He wished to learn all that he could before his own arrest. This no doubt was imminent. That of his wife had, of course, come as a shock to him, although he took it calmly like a true patriot, and by the time he arrived at the cottage he appeared his usual cheery self. He was truly elated in the thought that the Germans had not got Heath, and said that without him they could not prove anything against himself or against his wife.

The Belgian—I forget his name—and his wife would have let Heath remain at their cottage for as long as he wished, but both he and Neusy thought it best to leave and join me at Marie Godart's at the Sentier des Bonniers, although on arriving there, of course, they found that I had flown. So they stayed at Marie Godart's for the night and, as the reader already knows, joined me at La Bouverie the following morning.

From Grandma Godart's, Neusy sent out scouts to discover as far as possible all that had happened during his absence, and someone managed to see Jeanne and obtain her story, and also find out what the police had taken away from his house. So now in possession of all the facts, he decided to go to German headquarters at Mons with the air of an injured innocent, protesting against his wife's arrest and the confiscation of his property and cash. When he arrived, he was, of course, immediately arrested and kept in custody with his wife. This was only to be expected. After two days, however, the Germans told him that, apart from being in possession of German war material and rationed foodstuffs, they would not make any other charge against him, and keeping his money as bail for his appearance in court to answer these charges in due course, they now released him. They refused to tell him the charges they were making against his wife, but gave him to understand that they were serious.

Neusy knew that his release was a ruse on the part of the German police. They would now shadow him constantly in the hope that he would give away the whereabouts of the English soldiers, but they were up against a man who was far more intelligent and quicker on the uptake than they were themselves, and for the next two weeks he led his shadowers long walks in the country. At times his movements were so rapid and eccentric that they lost sight of him altogether, and whenever this happened, they would call again and again at his house, until they found him in, with the excuse that they must question him further in connection with the charges against his wife. But they could not hoodwink

I

Neusy. He knew that the object of their visit was to see if he was still in the village. He merely laughed up his sleeve at those Germans!

Throughout this long game of hide-and-seek Neusy was very careful to avoid the vicinity of the Sentier des Bonniers and La Bouverie. Nevertheless, although he kept well away from it, he daily sent messages to us, and to Marie Godart, so as to keep us informed as to how things were shaping.

9

Trial of Mme Neusy

LA BOUVERIE, like the village of Wasmes, lay in a depression, and consisted then of one long narrow street with a few additional houses behind. These were approached by alleys, deep in mud, and littered with garbage, old iron, and all the useless junk that people throw away.

Grandma Godart's house was situated half-way down this street. The front part of it had been converted into a shop. There she sold anything and everything, doing a fairly brisk trade, as it was the only shop of its kind in the village. Her only other occupation appeared to be chasing children who came to steal the dandelions she cultivated on a piece of grassland at the back of her house. For a lady of eighty she was very active, and it was a sight to see her running after them brandishing a big stick and calling out: 'Thieves! Thieves!' This could happen at least three times a day, but in spite of these raids she always seemed to have plenty of dandelions for her own needs. And good salads she used to make! I enjoyed them, and I often wonder why the dandelion is so scorned by the average English housewife. She does not know how good a thing she's missing!

It was a very subdued Heath now living at La Bouverie. Gone was his cheery optimism, and his mind was sorely troubled by the thought of what might happen to Marie Neusy. Indeed, of the two I now seemed to be the more cheerful, and I was happy in the thought that, in leaving the

Rue Calvier on the Mayor's warning, I had been proved right. No amount of argument could now disprove that, and, so far as Marie's arrest was concerned, my conscience was clear.

The days seemed long for both of us, and little happened to brighten our existence. Occasionally we got out of our rut by making fun of Grandma. When she was laying the table for the evening meal, we would put the things back in the cupboard as fast as she took them out without her seeing it, which was not difficult when the only source of light in the house was a cheap paraffin lamp of doubtful candle power. This would go on until Grandma commenced muttering to herself, 'Surely I got out so and so. Wherever is it?' Then one of us would burst out laughing, and Grandma would box our ears, and then sink into her armchair laughing too, often as not sitting on something eatable that one of us had put there on purpose! These little tricks were not very kind to an old lady, but they caused us all a little innocent merriment, and this would stop us thinking and worrying too much while we were waiting for Marie's trial.

Amongst Grandma's stock-in-trade were cereals. These drew rats to the house in their hundreds, and another occasional distraction with us was a rat hunt. The shop was closed to customers. Then everything on the floor was lifted up on to the benches which ran round it. Having done this, all the holes, except one, were blocked, and a few tempting bits of food scattered about on the floor in the centre of the room to entice them out, one of us standing beside the open hole with a mop ready to close it up when enough had emerged. Then we would cut off their retreat and account for them with sticks.

We were well guarded at La Bouverie against any surprise by the Germans. The shop was the only one in the street to sell sweets, and it was natural that this should be the spot where the children elected to play. Belgian children, like those of other nationalities, love a game of soldiers, and decorated with paper hats and wooden swords, they would march round and round, chanting a song that to me sounded something like:

Oop la! Oop la! Petit soldat.
Donner de la soupe, la!
Pour petit soldat.

This would go on hour after hour, until one of them would spot a solitary German or a party of them approaching from one end of the street or the other. Then, with all the strength of his lungs, he would yell out, '*Allemands! Allemands!*' Whereupon every child bolted for his home, just like our rats for their holes. Their panic was now our signal to watch from both the back and front of the house for any movement of the enemy to suggest that he was about to raid or search the village, but during the whole time we were at La Bouverie no alarm ever proved to portend anything of this kind.

A constant visitor to the house was the old lady's granddaughter, a girl of sixteen named Irma, and for some unknown reason she took a passionate liking for me at first sight, and showed it in no uncertain manner. I told her that I was married, but this made no difference. I just could not shake her off, and she continued to make every possible excuse for continually visiting her grandmother, and her attentions rendered my position almost embarrassing at times. I was, of course, afraid to offend her openly, for fear that she would give us away, and in the circumstances was forced to pretend to return her affections to some extent. Grandma herself noticed this, and warned me that Irma was really only a child. But I told her of my fears in relation to the Germans, and assured her that, so far as Irma was concerned, she had nothing whatever to worry about.

The thoughts of both of us were, of course, continually with Marie Neusy awaiting her trial at Mons. We longed for news of her, and in spite of the vigilance of her gaolers she did succeed in passing one written message out to Heath through her sister who was allowed to visit her. This said that she was quite happy, and that we were not to worry on her account. What she had done was done, not for us, but for her country. These were brave words, coming from a woman who might be sentenced to a long term of imprisonment or even to death. Then at last, after many weary days of waiting, we heard from Neusy that the date had been fixed for the trial. Heath and I, with heavy hearts, now anxiously awaited the result.

On the day of it we learned that she was charged with harbouring British soldiers in her house, a charge that, if proved, carried the death sentence. We knew, however, that the Germans really had little if any evidence with which to support this accusation. Neusy was called first, and questioned about *The Times Supplement* found in his house. This he tried to explain away by saying that he must have bought something in Brussels which had been wrapped up in it. He could not read English, he said, and could not account for it in any other way. This was a somewhat unconvincing explanation however, and it is clear that the Germans did not believe it. Indeed, the prosecution contended that an English newspaper in the house proved that Englishmen must have been hiding there.

The next witness called was Jeanne. She was invited to tell the court all she knew about the two English soldiers who had been hidden and looked after so well at the house in the Rue Calvier. But she would not have this. She indignantly denied that she had ever seen any English soldiers in the house or elsewhere. The prosecutor then snapped her up with the remark:

'Well, what about the one who escaped on the morning that your mistress was arrested? Now then, tell the truth, if you do not want to go to prison. We know all about it, for we caught him a week ago.'

'Yes,' she replied, 'I will tell you all about it.'

At this the Germans sat up and took notice. At last they were to hear something that would convict Marie Neusy of the charge against her. But Jeanne, child though she was, was playing with them. With a frightened glance towards Emile Neusy, she commenced her evidence, and maintained without hesitation that the man who was in the house on the day that her mistress was arrested was a Belgian whose Christian name was François. His surname she had never heard. Further, she stated that he was Mme Neusy's lover. He had been coming to the house for the last twelve months on almost every occasion when her master had been away on business. On the very morning of her mistress's arrest she had taken them coffee while they were in bed together!

A hush fell on the court, the Germans looking at one another, wondering whether after all there might not be some truth in this story. Or was she intentionally misleading them? This gave the Neusys, man and wife, time to think, and both decided simultaneously to bring into play that art of acting in which they both excelled. Neusy appeared at first to be stunned by what he had just heard. His wife hung her head. Then Neusy burst out into a torrent of abuse of his wife for her infidelity, and, thumping the table with his fist, demanded an immediate divorce. Indeed, he played the part of the wronged husband so well that he convinced the Germans that the girl's story was true, and they came to the conclusion that the report of English soldiers in the house was merely local gossip. So, after the court had adjourned for half an hour, Marie Neusy was brought in to be informed that the charge against her of sheltering British soldiers had been dropped. She was merely charged with impeding the police and resisting arrest, for which she was now sentenced to one month's imprisonment with hard labour. Neusy himself then answered the charge of being in possession of war material and rationed foodstuffs, and was heavily fined. The court also made him pay the whole cost of his wife's trial. These, together with his fines, added up almost to those seven hundred francs which had been confiscated by the Germans.

What a trial! And what a result! The methodical and machine-like mind of the German police had been upset by the wits of a thirteen-year-old Belgian girl whose pluck and insistence on sticking to her story in spite of threats had saved her mistress, and perhaps her master, from being shot for the crime of hiding English soldiers. But who was it who had betrayed Marie Neusy in the first instance? That I have thought about a lot. Clearly it must have been someone who knew the family intimately, someone who knew that three rings on the bell would signify the arrival of friends. The house had never been watched. I am positive of that. The street was continually under observation from the Neusys' house, and also from those of their immediate neighbours, and a watcher would have been spotted before he had been in position many minutes. It was also impossible for anyone to have heard the door bell from the street. Bearing all these facts in mind, I can only fix the guilt on Geoffrey Litard. He put the Germans, I am certain, on our track as an act of revenge against Heath, although at this time he probably did not realise the possible consequences of his act in respect of the woman he undoubtedly admired.

10

Escape organisation

A FEW days later Marcel Godart came over to La Bouverie with a message to the effect that we were to return to the Sentier des Bonniers with him after dark that night. Someone was coming to see us in connection with helping us to get back to England! This did not please Irma, and she accused me of loving her aunt (Marie Godart) more than I did her. For us it was the good news which we had been awaiting for months. Now, perhaps, we would at last hear something of that organisation which had hitherto been a myth so far as we were concerned. Leon Philliperon, it was true, had spoken of it in a vague sort of way, and we now wondered whether he might not be the person who was coming to see us on the morrow.

The unexpected result of the trial followed closely by Marcel's good news raised our hopes to a high level. It was difficult to be patient waiting, but at length it was dark enough to start, and we left La Bouverie in the company of Marcel, and reached the Sentier des Bonniers without incident, where we found old friends gathered at Marie Godart's house to welcome us. This included the postmaster and his wife, and later that evening I met the old man from the cottage next door whom Marie had previously dreaded, lest he should discover that she was hiding British soldiers. As already stated, I found him both interesting and genial, and never found out why she had ever been suspicious of him.

Before going to bed I tried hard to discover who it was who was coming to see us next day but Marie would not let on. Except that she said it was someone whom I already knew well, she would not tell me a word. So I went to bed wondering. Marie could be very close when she liked, but as the secret appeared to her to be a happy one, I was content to let her keep it to herself for the next few hours.

Early the next morning the long-expected visitor arrived, the one man, I think, of whom we had not thought! It was none other than M. Capiau, the engineer from the colliery hospital, and we both felt a little ashamed to meet him after the dirty trick we had played on him by running away and leaving him to 'carry the baby'. Our escapade was apparently forgotten however, anyhow as far as he was concerned, and he soon put us completely at our ease. He told us that an organisation now existed for the purpose of getting men like ourselves safely out of the country into Holland. We should be supplied in due course with identity cards, he said, and guided from place to place until we reached the frontier. He took our photographs there and then, saying that he hoped to have us on the move within ten days. So Heath and I began to picture ourselves back in good old England almost already. Little did we realise then what we had still got to go through before that happy day arrived.

This being the first time we had seen Capiau since our escape from the hospital, which was now nearly six months ago, he had much to tell us about what happened there on that eventful morning after we disappeared. We were not missed, he said, until about eight, and then within a few minutes every Belgian in the place was in a panic, fearing German reprisals for their negligence and clutching at the hope that we would be found at the Neusys', caught and brought back before the arrival of the German escort which was to have taken me to Germany. When we were not found there, for reasons the reader already knows, and when my escort did arrive at 10 a.m., the Belgian hospital authorities made a pretence of searching the colliery for me and, as they could not find me, swore black and blue that I had been seen only thirty minutes previously! So the Germans sent out patrols in all directions to try to catch us, and during the whole of that day M. Capiau and his staff were bullied with questions by the Commandant from St Ghislain, the same gentleman who had been so keen on sending me to Stettin-on-Oder for the beautiful fresh air of which, he thought, I so badly stood in need. They also questioned my old friend the wounded Prussian N.C.O. He maintained that he was entirely unaware of our absence. He even went so far as to swear that I had actually replaced one of his bandages as late as eight o'clock that morning! This lie helped to clear the Belgians, if it did not help me, and there was only one man in the colliery who could have disproved this statement, and in doing so have let everybody down. That was the stoker, who had lost his Sunday suit and had, of course, been causing trouble ever since he discovered his loss when he came off duty at 6 a.m. No one had thought, however, of linking up that theft with our escape until the latter was actually discovered, and then he was quickly given the money to buy a new suit, and sent home in haste, in case his loss reached the ears of the Germans. That might have led to serious trouble.

When after two days Heath and I had not been caught, the Germans got really furious, and threatened to take five of the principal citizens of Wasmes and hold them as hostages against our return. Fines galore were also levied on all Belgians who had any connection with the hospital, and things began to look black for all concerned. Further, a guard was now placed on the hospital, and daily inspections soon sent many patients away to German prison camps.

Then, on the third day after our departure, a new commandant took over, and he found the official list of patients in a
hopeless mess. It did not agree with the hospital records, the
old commandant's clerk having evidently kept rather bad
ones, probably deliberately. Still, it's an ill wind that blows
no one any good, and a little judicious monkeying with the
hospital records by Capiau made matters even worse with the
result that eventually the very existence of Heath and myself
began to be doubted by the new commandant. In the end
he accepted Capiau's revised list of patients as official. Our
escape had died a natural death, and was gradually forgotten!

Three or four days after his visit to the Sentier des
Bonniers Capiau, true to his promise, sent along our identity
cards. These were, of course, forgeries or, I should say, the
particulars on them were forgeries, i.e. imaginary names,
domiciles and occupations; and he had actually forged our
'signatures' without even having seen them! The cards themselves, with the official stamp on them, had been purloined
from the local German office.[1]

These cards gave us a queer feeling. By being in possession
of them we had, to all intents and purposes, changed our
nationality from British to Belgian, and yet neither of us
could really speak French well enough to have passed as a
native had we been questioned. I also carried my death
warrant on the upper part of my left arm in the form of a

1. I only learnt after the war how Capiau obtained these cards. He
had a friend who was employed as caretaker in the Town Hall of
Wasmes, and he kept him supplied with blank cards as required.
Capiau would then fill them in, and attach photographs which he had
taken of the prospective holders, and return them to the caretaker, who
would then get back to the Town Hall after the office had been closed
and stamp them with the official police stamp of Wasmes. This stamp,
partly covering the photograph of the holder, and the forged signature
of the Chief of Police, made these faked identity cards look in order.
                                                              Author

tattooed replica of the good old Union Jack! With this hall-mark of my nationality indelibly stamped on my body, my case would have been hopeless had I ever fallen into German hands.

Nine days after our return to Marie Godart's, true to his word again, Capiau informed us by messenger that a guide would pick us up early next morning to take us into Brussels. So that night a farewell party was arranged for us at the Sentier des Bonniers. All the Godarts were there, including Grandma and Irma, even the old man from next door, and, of course, my old friend the postmaster. We went to bed late, and early next morning our guide arrived, accompanied by the postmaster. The latter had been round some of his friends collecting money on our behalf, and now, with great ceremony, handed Heath and myself forty francs each, enclosed in a canvas wallet, as a farewell gift from friends in the village of Wasmes, many maybe friends whom we had never actually met.

Saying goodbye to the Godarts was a painful affair. All were in tears, as they kissed us farewell, and Grandma took a rosary from her neck, which she had worn ever since she was a child, and implored me to take it as a talisman against ill-luck and as something by which to remember her. As I am not a Catholic, a rosary had no particular significance for me. So, gently replacing it on the old lady's neck, I told her that I needed no reminder of her kindness. That would remain indelible in my memory as long as life should last.

Eventually we managed to make a start and, as Heath and I had nothing but the clothes in which we stood, we were not troubled by having to carry luggage. Our guide was an old man. He said we were to catch a tram that would get us to Mons in time to catch the bi-weekly steam tram to Brussels, and maintained that he knew a short cut to a place where we could catch it. So we took his short cut. An hour and a half passed, and we were still looking for the place where we were supposed to catch the tram. The old man had clearly lost his way, and, consulting his watch, now ruefully informed us that it would be impossible to catch it that day. This meant that we would have to wait another three days before we could make a fresh start! Heath and I had been looking forward to this day for months, and our failure to get away through no fault of our own was, to say the least of it, very disappointing.

During our trek across country that morning we came across the graves of many British and Germans who had fallen during the retreat, and were impressed by the fact that in many instances British and Germans were buried side by side. All graves had wooden crosses at their heads on which the particulars of those buried beneath were shown, the only distinction between British and German being a wreath of laurels on each cross under which a German lay. Most of the British graves, so far as I can remember, belonged to a fusilier regiment.

Our guide, if he can be so called, now suggested that we should return to Marie Godart's house, but neither of us felt that we could stand a repetition of the heart-rending scene that had taken place at our departure that morning, and, thoroughly disgusted with the situation, we sat down to talk it over. Finally we decided to try the Demoustiers. We felt sure that we should be welcome there for two or three days anyhow, and having settled that, and made sure that our guide knew where they lived, we set off in that direction. Their house, we knew, was only a few doors away from the Neusys', and our decision to return to the Rue Calvier was probably unwise, but, as their house could be entered from open country via the garden gate, it would not be difficult, we thought, to get in without anyone except the Demoustiers being aware of our return.

On arriving within sight of it Heath and I hid behind a slag-heap while our guide knocked up Mme Demoustier. We had arranged with him that, if everything was O.K., he should wave a white handkerchief from the garden gate, and after a few minutes the expected signal came. Heath and I now entered the house singly and at five-minute intervals and, as we had expected, found Mme Demoustier delighted to be our hostess for as long as we wanted to stay. She said she was particularly glad to have us as she so missed her son, Maurice, who had gone to the war, and that it would be some consolation to her to have two more sons, on whom she could lavish her affection, even if that were only for a day or two. Such was her attitude towards us! Before our guide left we asked him to report our whereabouts to Capiau, and to say that we would remain where we were until we got further instructions.

When M. Demoustier returned from business that night he was very surprised to find Heath and myself installed in his house. Like his wife, he was delighted to have us however, and showed it by buzzing round and suggesting all sorts of things for our comfort. Indeed, our stay with these people, short as it was, is for me a happy memory. We were treated like royal guests, and given of their best. They put us in their finest room, and this contained what must have been, at that time, the most up-to-date bedstead that had ever been invented. It was fitted with small flanged wheels, which ran on little rails, so that it could be pushed to the other side of the room without effort while cleaning the floor of grained and varnished oak. I had never seen a bed of this kind before. Nor have I ever seen another like it since.

After the affair at the Neusys' the Germans had been active searching the district, but their raids, like everything else they did, were so methodical that the inhabitants, by keeping a rough time-table, could almost foretell the day when their particular street would get their attention. All the same we had to keep a sharp look-out in case by any chance the police altered their routine. Meanwhile we waited anxiously for Capiau to come along again.

He turned up on the fourth night after our arrival at the Demoustiers', and led us away for some unknown destination, telling us *en route* that this time we really would get to Brussels. As we were travelling in the direction of the Sentier des Bonniers however, I quite thought that he was taking us back to Marie Godart. Indeed, my supposition seemed confirmed when, a little later, we actually crossed the road towards her house. So my surprise can be imagined when, instead of entering it, we were led through the gate of the adjoining château! The nature of those mysterious comings and goings, which I had observed from my attic window, was to be revealed at last!

A knock at the door by Capiau led a tiny panel in it to be opened, and someone to enquire who was there. Without hesitation Capiau spoke one word, which I did not catch, but it must have been a password. The heavy door was now opened by a lady of ample proportions. She bade us enter. We passed down a corridor to a large room. There we were introduced to eight more British soldiers, all, as a matter of fact, Irishmen, who had just arrived from the north of France and were being fitted out with suits, hats and boots. Heath and I were also invited to help ourselves to whatever we required in this line but, when we saw that all the suits were made of the same material and were of the same colour, and that all the hats were black Homburgs, we naturally declined. For, when those Irishmen were dressed up, they looked so uniform that anyone with half an eye could have seen that there was something suspicious about them as a party. Heath and myself felt safer in our old togs. I badly needed a new pair of boots but, owing to the fact that the

My forged identity card

Top left:
The Princess Marie de Croy

Top right:
Ada Bodart

SOME OF THE 'CONSPIRATORS'

Left:
Edith Cavell

address of Lieut. T's sister in England was hidden under the lining of one of my old ones, I could not possibly abandon them.

The mystery of the château was now solved. It was the headquarters and clearing house of this escape organisation, and the girls and women I had seen entering from time to time were guides for the men who were escaping. How strange that I should have lived for so long so near and yet so far from it, and that Marie Godart, who, one would have thought, knew everything that was going on, was ignorant of its existence! This only shows how secret and well guarded the activities of this organisation remained.

After a meal the whole party left the château in the company of Capiau. He took us to a café in the village of Pâturages, and there we met the guide who was to take us to Brussels the following morning. Naturally we all felt much excited at the thought that we might be in England in a few days. Heath and I, however, were not making the mistake a second time of counting our chickens before they were hatched. As subsequent events were to prove, it was a good thing that we did not!

We spent the night at the café, and next morning the whole party were up with the lark. Breakfast over, we left Pâturages, following our guide in couples some distance apart. After an hour and a half we reached the outskirts of Mons, which most of us had heard much about but few of us actually seen. The German occupation was much in evidence. There were German soldiers in their field-grey uniforms everywhere, and sentries posted on hotels, bridges and other places of importance. Most of the latter were old men with beards, and wore a peculiar type of headgear resembling, I thought, that worn by British infantry at Waterloo. Nevertheless, we reached the steam tram which was to take us into Brussels without being questioned. This

K

was a cumbersome affair, and its dilapidated appearance suggested that it must have been built not long after Stephenson's *Rocket*.

Boarding it seemed to me like the beginning of another new adventure, and I did so half in fear and half in delight, full of thoughts of what I hoped, if all went well, might really lie ahead. We sat in it for some time. Then after much clanging and snorting it started, travelling at a speed of about six miles an hour. Half-way to Brussels it stopped, and in jumped the German police, demanding '*Papiers! Papiers!*' in gruff, bullying voices. Keeping our eye on our guide, who sat in front, we saw that this merely meant showing our identity cards, but as it was the first time that I had had to show mine, I felt nervous lest the policeman should ask me any awkward questions, to which I would have to reply in French, or discover that my identity card was really a forgery. My hands trembled, as I handed it over to him, but to my great relief he just compared the photograph on it with my own face, and then handed it back without comment. The eight Irishmen all dressed alike, and sitting together in the tram, looked to me remarkably suspicious, but the Germans never seemed to notice it. This was lack of observation and intelligence on their part which one would not have expected from a British policeman.

Just before we got under way again two German officers jumped on and sat down uncomfortably close to me. I endeavoured to look out of the window, as if quite unconcerned. In reality I felt anything but happy. My stomach turned over and over, as if it was tying itself in knots, but in a few minutes, to my very great relief, they shifted their seats to the front compartment. I suppose it was natural to feel afraid when coming into contact with the Germans on our first day's journey. This feeling soon passed off, however. In a few days I had seen so many Germans, even sat next to several, that I got quite used to being among them. Indeed, I soon realised that there was no need to fear the German in uniform, simply because one knew he was a German. It was the other German, the secret policeman in mufti, who was the dangerous fellow. The country, if the Belgians were to be believed, was now permeated with these chaps. They were everywhere, prying into the homes and affairs of its inhabitants, and continually bringing charges against these unhappy people, most of them false and trumped up, merely to justify their own cushy existence. No wonder that the Belgians were very wary of conversation with any stranger. A fugitive British soldier had to be careful indeed.

Later in the afternoon our tram arrived at its destination, the Place Pouppe. Here our party alighted, and followed our guide by a devious route through the cobblestone streets of Brussels until we were ushered into a hospital clinic in the Rue de la Culture. Here we were surprised to be welcomed by an Englishwoman who appeared to be in charge. We had not expected that! She showed us a room, where the only light came through a skylight in the roof as it was matchboarded all round so that no prying eyes could peep in through windows, and which was plainly furnished with wooden tables and forms, scrubbed to a snowy whiteness, and heated by a typical Belgian stove standing in the centre of it. A dozen or so British soldiers waiting for an opportunity, they soon told us, to be guided to the frontier, were there already. Here, in fact, almost in the heart of Brussels, under the very nose of the enemy, someone had had the pluck and the nerve to form what could only be described as a concentration camp for British fugitives!

We were soon all talking. With the exception of four of us, all the men in the clinic at the moment proved to be Irishmen, belonging to the Munster Fusiliers. Time passed happily, and sometimes the lady herself would come and talk to us. What a pleasure it was for all us fugitives to sit round the fire listening to this countryman of ours, who in her pleasant, quiet and cultured voice would discuss the war, and the Germans, and tell us about the fugitives who had come and gone before us. We did not know the name of this little woman with her calm, grey eyes, at this time; and, if we had heard it, we would have paid no heed to it then. It was enough for us to know at that time that she was English, and that she really intended to help us. Only later did we all learn that this unassuming person was none other than the brave Nurse Edith Cavell!

As matron of a clinic she must have been a busy woman, but every moment that she could spare she seemed to spend in our company. We all looked forward to her visits. Further, realising that, cooped up in one room all day, we got no exercise, she gave us leave to go out in the evenings for walks, saying that she thought that would be quite safe, provided we left the clinic singly or in pairs, kept to the quiet thorough-fares, and refrained from ever speaking English in the hearing of other people. But we must play the game, she said, and be very careful. There were many German officers billeted in houses quite close to the clinic.

Although Nurse Cavell granted this privilege, she told me personally that she would much rather we never went out at all, and I never did go out, but as we were not prisoners she said that she had no right to keep us in against our will. Anyhow, all who went out were expected to return by 9 p.m. at the latest, the time at which the wards were shut down for the night. Nor was there any doubt about the Germans being billeted in the immediate vicinity. When our lights were out, and we pulled up the blinds, we could see them through the French windows of the houses at the back of the clinic, playing cards and drinking.

On the third night after our arrival I regret to say that we had serious trouble. Nine o'clock, then ten o'clock came, but only two of the Irishmen had returned. Something must have happened to the rest! Miss Cavell was perturbed, some of her nurses were almost in a panic, and an English doctor, 'Dr B.', who, unknown to the Germans, came to the clinic to attend any of us who needed him, was furious. He bundled those of us who had not gone out, or who had already come back, into a small ward and locked the door.

Before long everyone knew what had happened. The Irishmen were young, raw and undisciplined, and had left the clinic in ones or twos, according to instructions, but had later either by design or accident (which I do not know) foregathered in a café some distance away. There they settled down to have a merry evening. Soon some of them became the worse for drink and, as can always be expected from the Irishman, a fight of some kind was soon in progress. Then, having caused some damage to the café, they were ejected, and now rolled back in a bunch singing *Tipperary* at the tops of their voices.

To me it seemed almost unbelievable that men of the British Army could have so far forgotten themselves for the sake of a drink, and their conduct, with Germans all round them, was crazy. They had placed themselves, Nurse Cavell, and all the many others who were working to save their lives, in the greatest danger, although, so far as I know, this incident passed unnoticed by the Germans. Those in charge of the clinic got in a panic, however, and as a precaution took drastic steps. We were roused before daylight next day and, after a hasty breakfast, told that we would be handed over to the guides who would distribute us among houses in the district belonging to people who were helping in the escape organisation.

We left the clinic as dawn was breaking, at intervals and in small groups, for our various destinations and, in the hurry and scurry of getting away, I became separated from my old comrade Heath. This was hard luck after we had been through so much together but, unfortunate as it was, one could not make one's own arrangements under the circumstances prevailing. Further, I was under the impression that the move was temporary, and that we should all meet again back at the clinic in a few days when the scare had blown over. In this assumption I was wrong. None of us ever returned to Miss Cavell's after that unhappy incident.

I now found myself paired up with an Irishman named Michael Carey of the Munster Fusiliers, the sole survivor of a party of twelve Munsters who had been sheltered by the miller at Hiron and who, in return for his kindness to them, had worked his mill and tilled his land until, suddenly at dawn one morning, the mill had been raided by the Germans. Eleven of them, and the miller himself, had then been tried on the spot, condemned to death, and shot within the space of an hour. The mill and its outhouses had been burnt to the ground, and the miller's wife and family transported to Germany. Such was the drastic and vicious punishment inflicted by the Germans on Belgians who were found sheltering British soldiers out of the goodness of their hearts.

Michael Carey, as I have said, was the sole survivor of this tragedy, and owed his life to the fact that on the night before the raid he had had a sudden inclination to leave his bed in the hayloft to visit friends on a neighbouring farm, and there he had stayed for the night, to return next morning to find what had been his home for many months a smoking ruin, and to learn of the unhappy fate that had overtaken the miller and all his comrades. This moved Michael Carey to such an extent that, an ardent Catholic himself, he fell on his knees in full view of many of the local inhabitants who had gathered to the scene, and thanked his Maker for his own escape and prayed for the souls of his unhappy comrades.

Carey and I were now taken by a guide to a house in the Avenue Longchamps, the home of M. Séverin, a well-known Brussels chemist. His wife, Madame Séverin, was a gigantic woman, but very charming, and hated the Boche like poison. She could only refer to any German as a *sale bête*. However, from the first day of our arrival we shared the hospitality of the Séverins with that of the people next door. I cannot remember their name now. The husband was a man of small stature, and a tailor by profession. His happiest moment was when he was entertaining us on his piano, with the grace and air of a Paderewski, while his wife and Mme Séverin were quarrelling as to who was to have the privilege of feeding us next day. Such was the hospitality of these wonderful people belonging to this organisation which was trying to help British soldiers still at liberty. They must have known the penalty they might incur, but their patriotism and love of the British soldier inspired them to carry on, without thought of self, in face of the risk of being caught by the German secret police who were now working underground throughout the country that their government was striving to control.

Abortive attempt

O N APRIL 6th, after we had been at the Avenue de Longchamps for seven days, a guide arrived to pick us up to make an attempt to cross the frontier at a spot near Turnhout in the north of Flanders. He introduced himself as Louis Declassé, which I knew was an assumed name. I am pretty sure he was not one of Miss Cavell's guides but we did not know who had sent him. He was a nervous man with shifty eyes, and I felt instinctively that I could not really trust him.

At about 7 a.m. Carey and I said goodbye to our friends in the Avenue de Longchamps, and set out for the Église St Marie, where we hoped to get a tram for at least some part of our journey, and on the way we picked up, from the house of another member of the organisation, four of the Irishmen who had caused so much trouble at the clinic. The fact that these men were joining our party, coupled with my impression of Declassé, made me very dubious of the outcome of our venture.

On arriving at the church we successfully boarded the tram. I say successfully because it was something of a struggle. It was crowded with fat, greasy German soldiers. They occupied all the seats and most of the standing room. We poor fugitives had to hang on by the skin of our teeth, and what was so annoying, too, was that, while these Germans travelled free, we fugitives had to pay our fares!

Before the tram had travelled two miles most of the Germans got off, leaving us almost its only occupants. Twenty minutes later we passed through a fair-sized village where, as we left it, I saw two tremendous hangars situated in and partly hidden by a grove of willow trees, and, as we drew further away, I could see the nose of two Zeppelins protruding from the other side of them. I asked Declassé the name of the village through which we had just passed. He told me that it was Evere, and I made a mental note of this, intending to report it, if I ever really had the luck to get back to Blighty.[1]

We left the tram at 10 a.m., and continued our journey on foot, walking in couples at intervals of about two hundred yards, Declassé striding on alone in front. At about midday we entered the ill-fated town of Louvain. German engineers were still busy repairing telegraph wires and lines, and we saw some of the results of the terrible outrage committed there by the Germans on the 25th August 1914.[2]

1. i.e. get home, Blighty being a common way in which to refer to the home country during the First World War. It originated with the Army serving in India as a corruption of the Hindustani word *Vilayet*, meaning the state. A 'Blighty one' was the kind of wound that got a man quickly and safely home, and many will remember the song:

> Tiddledy—iddledy—ighty
> Take me back to Blighty.
> Blighty is the place for me!
>
> *Editor*

2. Whenever the German Army met resistance they had turned on the civil population, the worst atrocities being committed at Louvain, Aerschot, Visé, and Tamines. Where they had been allowed to pass unopposed there was no organised burning and pillaging, and no massacres. Brussels was declared an open city and escaped completely, and the Belgians in the Borinage did not suffer at the hands of the Germans after the British retreat to anything like the same extent as after the retreat of their own army east of Brussels. In the Borinage there were no organised atrocities, no *Schrecklichkeit*. Brand Whitlock, *Belgium under German Occupation* (Heinemann, 1919). *Editor*

Leaving Louvain we trudged on, and during the afternoon passed through Aerschot and Diest, the former the site of another terrible atrocity. Both, too, showed signs of having been under terrific fire. The woodwork of the doors and windows had been splintered and pitted by bullets. Then, as daylight was failing, our guide left the road for open country, and by eight o'clock we arrived at the gates of the monastery of Averbode, situated in its own grounds and almost hidden from view by tall trees that grew all round it.[1] At the wicket gate we were met by a monk. He conducted us to the Father Superior, at least that is what I call him, who in turn took us over to a building attached to the laundry, the living quarters of the laundress and her daughter, the only women in the establishment. Here we sat down to a filling meal of bread, fat bacon, and coffee, after which we chatted with one of the monks who happened to be able to speak English. Meanwhile the table and forms were removed, and rough beds fitted up for us. So, apologising for cutting short our conversation with our English-speaking friend, who would, I believe, have gone on talking all night, we lost no time in getting into them. We were all in need of a good night's rest.

Next morning we were up early, breakfasted quickly, and were ready for the road by five. As we left the monastery Declassé enquired if we had any objection to a young Belgian, who wanted to cross the frontier, joining us. Of course we had no objection. So our party now numbered eight, and we walked in couples, the Belgian in front with Declassé. Soon we left the main road, and continued along tracks across open country. Everything went on swimmingly until about noon. Then we came to a railway crossing, and

1. An abbey of the Premonstranasian Order, founded in 1136, pillaged in 1514, but its church rebuilt on a magnificent scale and in the baroque style in 1670, and furnished with a famous organ. The abbey itself was restored in 1770, but largely destroyed by fire in 1942. The church escaped.

at this point a German sentry demanded our papers. Our first three pairs passed through without incident, but as the last two Irishmen came up, one of them had an attack of nerves, and could not remember into which pocket he had put his identity card, and fumbling about to find it, pulled out some other papers, among which were some 5-franc notes. Then, as he returned these to his pocket, one of the notes fluttered to the ground. Whereupon the sentry promptly put his foot on it, and then, looking over his shoulder towards the guard room to make sure that no one was looking, passed the Irishman on with a wave of his hand.

This delay led the three pairs in front to close up, and wait under cover of some undergrowth until the last had come up but, before they reached us, they suddenly started to fight! While the nervous man was searching for his identity card, his comrade had observed that he was in possession of some letters which he had apparently been carrying about ever since he left England! This had started an argument, which led to the fight, and when they reached us, and we learned the facts, the fool was stripped of every incriminating document he possessed, and these all torn up and burnt on the spot. How any man with any common sense could be such an idiot as to retain a few letters, endangering his own life and that of others, was beyond the comprehension of us all. How lucky he distracted the sentry's mind by dropping that five-franc note!

Early in the afternoon we struck the main road again and shortly afterwards came in sight of Turnhout. Our party was not the only one entering the town that day. There were many others, consisting mostly of young men. I asked Declassé who they all were, and he told us that all able-bodied men up to a certain age had to report to German headquarters in their district once a month to prove that they still remained in occupied territory. Failure to report meant that their parents or other relations would be fined or put in prison.

Whether it was by design or accident that we were on the road on the same day, and at the same time, as these other young men, I do not know. If it was by design, then it had been well thought out beforehand. For Turnhout, situated as it is very near the Dutch frontier, would have been very difficult to enter on any other day. There would have been strict examination of identity cards and awkward questions asked as to our business. As it was it proved easy. The Germans, thinking we were all civilians going in to report, just compared our photographs with our faces, and then let us pass without asking any questions.

On reaching the outskirts of the town our guide handed us over to the young Belgian who had accompanied us from the monastery, giving him instructions to take us to a certain address where we would find our next guide, the one who was to take us over the frontier during the night. Bidding us goodbye and good luck, Declassé now mounted the bicycle, which he had borrowed from the monastery and had been pushing all day, and rode off in the direction whence we had come.

Declassé's action in handing his job over to this young fellow, who was not much more than a lad, seemed to me suspicious, and confirmed my early impression that he was not to be trusted far. So in Turnhout I felt very unhappy, particularly as it was soon apparent to all of us that there were three times as many Germans in the streets as Belgians. Further, the movement of every Belgian was clearly being watched, and, nearing our destination, our temporary guide left us in the street, while he went on alone to find the house and make sure that the coast was clear. Standing in a group we soon became an object of curiosity to passing Germans.

We therefore split up and got moving, walking up and down, and occasionally stopping to gaze into shop windows.

For what seemed hours, although it was probably not really more than a matter of minutes, we paraded up and down in this way, keeping our eyes skinned for the return of our guide. At last we saw him turn the corner. But his face looked white and scared. Clearly something had gone very wrong and, without speaking or showing the least sign of recognising us, he passed by and made his way out of the town with all speed while we, with our hearts in our mouths, followed him at intervals of about fifty yards.

When we were clear of Turnhout he took us into a café, where there were no Germans, and as soon as we had all arrived told us what had happened. The house, to which he had been instructed by Declassé to take us, had proved to be occupied by German soldiers as a billet, and the Belgian, who had formerly lived there, and who was to have been our next guide, was not to be found. Further, although he had made enquiries of neighbours, nobody seemed to recognise the name of the man which had been given him by Declassé. Presumably it was a false name.

Our position was now clearly serious, and we all agreed that it would be dangerous to remain in the vicinity of Turnhout. Most of us in fact declared for returning to the monastery at Averbode. But our young Belgian friend was of different mind. He had come so far, and was reluctant to go back without at least having had a try to cross that frontier, and with this idea he left us in the café, and went out to try to find a guide of some kind who would take us over that night. In this he was unsuccessful, and when he returned an hour later he told us he had gathered that, to cross the frontier, we would have to dodge two chains of sentries and swim a canal which, without an experienced guide and as only two of our party could swim, would be impossible. These facts were sufficient to persuade him to take us back to Averbode.

The distance from Brussels to Turnhout is approximately sixty-five miles, and we had covered most of this on foot in forty-eight hours. That day alone we had trudged twenty-one miles on a chunk of bread and a piece of fat bacon, and one or two glasses of water for which we even had to pay! The Flemish never give anything away! So we were heartily fed up, footsore and weary, and none of us felt like walking another twenty-one miles if there were any means of transport. So, as our temporary guide said he might be able to find someone who could give us a lift back to the monastery, we sent him out in search, and he returned after about an hour, accompanied by an old woman, the proud possessor of a horse and ramshackle farm cart with a kind of hood over it. This old lady informed us that she had a permit to carry passengers, and that she would take us to Averbode for twelve francs a head. We pooled our money on the café table, and, when it was counted, it totalled a hundred and five francs, out of which we paid her eighty-seven francs. This she insisted on taking home before we started, leaving us the horse and cart behind as her guarantee of good faith. While she was gone we spent the balance of our money on food and coffee to fortify ourselves against the night.

At 9 p.m. we started on a journey that was to give me one of the biggest frights of my life. The floor of the cart was covered with straw. This was at once claimed by the five Irishmen, although how they all found room to lie down in such a small space remained a mystery to me. They were welcome to it however. With my usual inclination to be in a position to see and hear what was going on, I much preferred to sit in front.

The night was cold, and the north-easterly wind penetrated my very bones. My feet were wet, and I was insufficiently clad. Before we had been on the road an hour I was frozen. Further, I felt depressed and disappointed at our failure and, as the old cart rumbled along over the uneven road, I felt that it would be better to die, and so end all one's troubles! Only the misery of that journey kept me wide awake.

Months of watching, waiting, and listening, had developed my sense of hearing to a high degree. I could not only hear the slightest sound, but was able to guess the probable nature of it with uncanny accuracy. This was lucky. Suddenly, as we approached a part of the road which was fringed by tall trees, I heard a faint sound in the distance, undoubtedly metallic. I listened carefully, and heard it again. Surely it was a restless horse champing its bit? And that could only mean a German mounted patrol! So I woke up my Irish companions, and told them to get ready. Trouble, I was certain, loomed in the offing. My fears were soon confirmed. A few yards further on we were suddenly pulled up by a short sharp '*Halten!*' Next moment a German officer walked out from behind the trees, and I was half blinded by the glare of an electric torch thrust into my face.

He now commenced yelling at me in Flemish, a language of which I hardly understand a word, and as my eyes got used to the light of his torch, I saw that in his other hand he held an automatic pistol with the business end not more than three inches from my head. It was a bad moment. My heart gave a jump, stopped, and then started racing fast enough to burst my ribs. My hair stood on end, and my mouth went dry. I was, in fact, 'scared stiff'. Meanwhile the officer continued to yell at me but I would have been quite unable to answer him, even if I had understood a word of his questions. Mercifully at this point the old woman came to my rescue, and started to argue with him, as the result of which we were soon all ordered off the cart and lined up by the side of the road. Our pockets were now searched, and our identity cards examined, while all the time the old woman and our young guide kept up a vociferous argument with the officer and the N.C.O. with him. This at least prevented them from putting further questions to us. Eventually everything seemed to have been settled satisfactorily, and we were allowed to proceed on our way!

What a narrow shave for us all! That officer must have been very new at his job. There were many suspicious things about us which he failed to realise. There were discrepancies in our credentials which escaped his notice. We were many miles away from the district of our registration, even if our identity cards had been genuine. We were abroad during prohibited hours. We had no special permit to travel by night. Only two of the party had replied to his questions. No doubt darkness helped us, and the fact that we were travelling away from the frontier, instead of towards it, tended to eliminate suspicion. What a prize that officer had missed! Six British Tommies! Their capture would have brought him promotion. Was it luck or providence that saved us? Which was it, too, that had brought those letters in the Irishman's pocket to light less than twenty-four hours before this incident? They would have certainly been our undoing.

During the rest of the journey, which was happily without further incident, the Belgian related to me the gist of the conversation which had taken place between him, the woman, and the officer. The old woman had protested vehemently against the indignity of being pulled up while conveying honest men into Brussels to collect stores for the starving population of Turnhout! She, of course, did not know our real identity. Her protest was genuine. Our guide had told her this story in order to induce her to cart us to Averbode. So she remained supremely unaware of the good

Top left:
Prince Réginald de Croy

Top right:
Brother Michael Appermans

MORE OF THE 'CONSPIRATORS'

Left:
Philippe Baucq

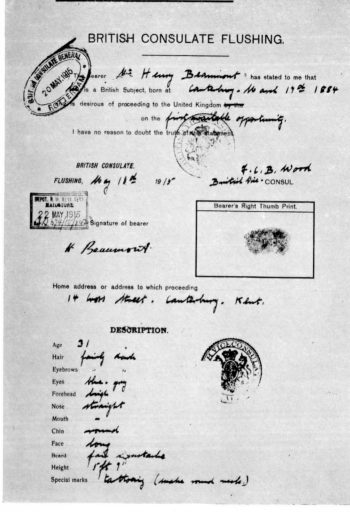

Available for one journey only.

BRITISH CONSULATE FLUSHING.

The bearer *Mr Henry Beaumont* has stated to me that he is a British Subject, born at *Canterbury. March 19th 1884* and is desirous of proceeding to the United Kingdom by the on the *first available opportunity.*

I have no reason to doubt the truth of this statement.

BRITISH CONSULATE.

FLUSHING, *May 18th* 19 *15*

F. C. B. Wood
British Vice-CONSUL.

Signature of bearer

H. Beaumont.

Bearer's Right Thumb Print.

Home address or address to which proceeding

14 North Street. Canterbury. Kent.

DESCRIPTION.

Age *31*
Hair *fairly dark*
Eyebrows *" "*
Eyes *blue. grey*
Forehead *high*
Nose *straight*
Mouth *-*
Chin *round*
Face *long*
Beard *fair moustache*
Height *5 ft 9"*
Special marks *tattooing (snake round neck.)*

My passport home

turn she had done us by not allowing that German officer to get a word in edgeways.

During the rest of the journey we stopped occasionally to listen for signs of being followed by that patrol. They were evidently satisfied however. They never followed us, and we arrived at the monastery about four in the morning, and were soon inside, horse, cart, old woman and all. Within half an hour, too, we were comfortably settled in bed in the laundress's quarters as before. A pity, it seemed, that these two hardworking women should have been put to such inconvenience, but they, like most Belgians who knew who we were, deemed it a privilege to make some sacrifice to help a British soldier.

Next morning, April 8th, we were roused by our temporary guide. He came to bid us goodbye, and before leaving promised to go to the clinic in the Rue de la Culture and report our failure to cross the frontier, and also to inform the matron of our present whereabouts. Then the English-speaking monk took us on a tour of the monastery. And a beautiful place it was! The carvings and the marble statuary were wonderful, and the corridors were hung with portraits of monks long since dead and gone. In one of the lecture rooms hung a huge map showing the war on the Eastern and Western fronts, the position of each army indicated by tiny national flags stuck into it with pins, forming snake-like lines. This was the first thing of its kind that we had seen, and although our position on the Western Front did not look very hopeful, it was interesting to us, who had lost all touch with the war, to get some idea as to how things really stood.

We were now taken to a room at the top of the building, and there we were fitted out as monks, complete with hoods, gowns, girdles and sandals. Our moustaches were shaved off, and our hair cut short, because, we were told, if we were going to stay at the monastery for any length of time, these

L

precautions were absolutely necessary. Germans occasionally came there to pay their religious devotions, and sometimes wandered about the buildings. If one turned up, we were all to kneel down and say our prayers! We were also told that we could use the room at the top of the building during the day. But we were to go on sleeping in the laundry at night.

After our first day there, we had great difficulty in finding much to do to pass the time. All we could think of was playing cards for buttons. We could not play for money for the simple reason that none of us had any. The Irishmen, including Carey, being Catholics, attended services in the chapel at every opportunity, and on these occasions I was left alone with my thoughts. These were full of thankfulness for the past, and for some reason, in spite of our many reverses, I began to get more hopeful about the future.

Days came and days went at the monastery, but still no guide came to take us back to Brussels, and the monks began to get anxious. It looked as if we were going to be on their hands much longer than they had thought. Nevertheless, they were very good to us, and we had plenty of food and a liberal supply of beer. This was brewed in the monastery, and being fairly strong tended to make the Irishmen quarrelsome, and sometimes anything but cheerful companions. Then, on April 13th, we learned that the English-speaking monk had left for Brussels, his object being to see Miss Cavell with a view to getting us away. The authorities at the monastery certainly thought that the organisation should send a guide to take us back to Brussels.

He returned the following evening with Declassé, the same guide who had let us down at Turnhout, and we learned from him that the young Belgian had never been anywhere near the clinic, and that the organisation had remained completely ignorant of our predicament. I do not know how much of this fiasco had really been Declassé's fault. Anyhow, he got severely 'told off' by Michael Carey, who spoke French like a native, for not having finished his job. I am afraid however that Carey's outburst was largely wasted on him. Declassé simply said that he was under the impression that everything had been in order, and that we had arrived safely in Holland.

12

Stranded

SEVEN days later we left the homely portals of the monastery to return to Brussels. This time we were lucky, and did most of the forty-two miles by tram. We met with few Germans, only showed our identity cards twice, and by 7 p.m. Carey and I were installed in a house in the Rue du Brasserie, the home of Mlle Dobie, a very wealthy and lively young Belgian woman of about thirty, and obviously an aristocrat. As we entered the house we had been struck by its luxury, and when she came down she greeted our guide with these words:

'What! Only two! That's a shame. You promised me at least six.'[1]

Declassé had left the other four outside. Why, or what became of them, I do not know. I never saw any of them again. They were good fellows in their way. Yet I was not sorry to be parted from them. Their Irish temperament made them a positive danger both to themselves and to anyone who was forced, under our circumstances, to live or travel in their company.

As soon as Declassé left, Mlle Dobie asked whether we

1. I have no idea who Mlle Dobie was, but she may have been the same lady as the Mlle Martin to whom Edith Cavell referred in her 'confession' as one of those who hid soldiers in Brussels. (See *Edith Cavell*, p. 160.)   *Editor*

would like a bath or would prefer to have dinner first? A bath! Did I really hear her aright? I had never yet seen a bath in Belgium, let alone had one! I had had one or two makeshifts. But those were baths by instalments, so to speak. Carey and I were hungry, but with this offer in view we could afford to wait for our supper. The luxury of a bath was the greatest attraction of all!

Whether I looked the dirtier, I do not know, but for some reason Mademoiselle selected me for the first one, and conducted me to my bedroom, where she left me while she prepared it. As the bathroom was only a few feet away, she chatted away in good English in the meanwhile, asking me to leave everything I took off in the bathroom. She would arrange to have my underclothes washed and my suit, such as it was, cleaned. The room belonged to her brother, she said, who was away at the war, and added:

'You'll find everything you need in the wardrobe. So, please help yourself.'

Not having had an opportunity to change my underclothes for weeks, I was carrying some unwelcome company, and not wishing Mademoiselle to handle my clothing, I was forced to tell her about it. She did not understand at first; in fact not until I scratched my ribs and exclaimed, 'Parasites'! 'Poor man!' she replied. 'I understand. Everything shall be burned.'

Having had my bath, which was indeed a luxury, and decked myself out in Mademoiselle's brother's clothes, which fitted me none too badly, I once again felt clean enough to mix with decent people, and, as I descended to the dining-room, she met me at the door, and ran her eyes over me with approval until she spotted my boots. Why had I not taken a pair from the wardrobe? So I had to tell her the story of Lieutenant T. and my promise to him. This brought tears to her eyes, and she begged me to take a pair of her brother's boots, and secrete his address in the lining of them. The following day she helped me to do this herself.

In the dining-room I found three other fugitives besides Carey: two Frenchmen and a mysterious fellow who claimed to be a Canadian. He said he was a reservist, and that he had been in London at the outbreak of the war, had volunteered for service with the British Army, and had come to France with the Fusiliers. He was very talkative but the two Frenchmen were supercilious, and would not speak to us Britishers unless we insisted on talking to them.

As soon as Carey had also had his bath, and fixed himself up in borrowed clothes, too, we all sat down to dinner, Mademoiselle apologising for what she described as a 'poor spread', although it consisted of beef and other good things, and champagne! If this was a poor spread, I would have liked to see one of her good ones! We could not have had a better dinner if we had been royal guests, instead of fugitive British soldiers, and while dinner was in progress our hostess told us what she would give us for breakfast on the morrow. 'It shall be a real English one,' she said, 'porridge, toast, marmalade, eggs and bacon.' Carey and I doubted whether such things were really to be had in Belgium. But she was as good as her word; and, when the time came, faithfully produced a truly British breakfast. She was wealthy, and almost anything could still be bought in Brussels by anyone who had money. In the meanwhile Carey and I had been sent to bed with a bottle of 'Black and White', and a syphon of soda water, just in case we were thirsty during the night!

In the dining-room we were shown a cupboard well stocked with wines, liqueurs and spirits; and during the day we were invited to help ourselves when we wanted a drink. The self-styled Canadian, whoever he was, took full advantage of this. He helped himself liberally, too. The result was that by noon he was often half drunk and in a very quarrelsome mood, and in this state would invariably pick upon me for an argument. I was the smallest of the party. He was a giant, nearly twice my size, and under these circumstances I thought discretion the better part of valour, and usually made a point of agreeing with everything he said. Even then he sometimes got nasty, and tried to bully me, until Carey, who stood over six feet, and would have been the much better man had it ever come to blows, told him to 'pack it up'. Then he saw the red light and shut up, retiring to a couch to sleep off the effects of his indiscretion.[1]

Even in his sober moments he was an awful liar. If he had performed half the brave deeds he claimed, he would have been entitled to the V.C. with at least a dozen bars. This boastfulness annoyed our hostess, and bored us beyond words. Carey and I soon became her favourites, much to the disgust of the Canadian and the Frenchmen, who had had the run of the place until we two arrived. Usually she talked to us in French, as she said we understood her French better than she understood our English. Indeed, she only resorted to English when she wanted to say something that she did not want the Frenchmen to hear. In the afternoon a lady friend of hers sometimes came in, and between them they taught Carey and myself to play bridge. It was a game quite new to us but, being used to many card games in the Army, we soon picked it up and became better at it than our tutors! While we were playing, the two Frenchmen would sit there looking like sulky children who felt that they were being left out of something.

Twice at the Rue de Brasserie we were visited by Philippe Baucq, the architect. He came clad in a long, black cloak

---

1. This lavish supply of food and drink surprised me, and I asked Beaumont about it. He said that it was like that. He had not exaggerated. If you were rich, or in the trade, you could get anything you wanted. Ordinary people had to go without.   *Editor*

clasped at the throat and, with a soft black wide-brimmed hat, looked the typical artist. On each occasion he entered by the French windows at the back of the house, and never stayed more than three minutes, giving the impression of a fearless man conscious that he was being shadowed. He was a great patriot and closely connected with *La Libre Belgique*, a newspaper secretly printed and distributed throughout occupied Belgium.[1]

When the day came, I was almost sorry to leave this house of luxury, where such food, cooked by someone whom we never saw, came up on a lift from the kitchen down below (our hostess kept three servants whose work was so arranged that we never saw them once during the ten days we were there), to begin taking risks again. But, as I say, that day did come, and on April 15th Carey and I and the two Frenchmen left for a destination unknown in charge of Declassé, in whom, it must be said, we had not got much confidence. The Canadian refused to accompany us, and we left him behind. What became of him I do not know.[2]

The order of march was the same as before, Declassé in

1. This clandestine paper was published in Brussels (and appeared each month on the German Governor General's table) in spite of many arrests, two courts martial, and every effort on the part of the Germans to suppress it, from February 1915 right up to the return of King Albert to his capital in November 1918. (See Oscar Millard, *Uncensored*, London, 1937.) *Editor*

2. This mysterious character may have been the Frenchman, Gaston Quien, who was serving a sentence for a civil offence at the outbreak of war and, when released, found himself in German-occupied territory. So he posed as a French officer, cut off at the battle of Charleroi, and was evacuated to Holland via the château at Bellignies and Miss Cavell's institute in Brussels. He came back across the frontier, however, and is said to have informed the German Police about Miss Cavell. After the war he was tried in Paris, and condemned to death, but his sentence was commuted to hard labour. (See *Edith Cavell*, p. 140 et seq.) He could well have masqueraded as a French Canadian. If he was not Quien, he was another such man taking similar advantage of the situation.—*Editor*.

front by himself, followed by us two, with the two Frenchmen
bringing up the rear. During the morning we successfully
passed through several examining posts by simply flourish-
ing our identity cards in the sentries' faces, and early in the
afternoon reached Malines, which showed signs of having
been badly knocked about by gun-fire. As soon as we were
clear of the town Declassé informed us that we were bound
for Antwerp, and all went well and without a hitch of any
kind until we came to a bridge over the Walhain Canal.
Here there was a sentry on each side of the road. Now in
every case where there were *two* sentries, our method was to
approach the post slowly, giving ourselves time to study both
of them in order to try to make up our minds as to which of
the two looked the least intelligent. On this occasion Carey
and I had no doubt about it at all. The one on the left wore
glasses and looked alert and inquisitive. The one on the right
was obviously of the peasant class, and looked dull and
stupid, and we decided to show our cards to him. He let us
pass without asking any questions. Then, about five hundred
yards up the road, as we turned a bend, we caught up with
Declassé and together we waited for the two Frenchmen.
We waited and waited, and when after twenty minutes to
half an hour there was still no sign of them, Declassé got
alarmed, and returned to the bridge to see what had
happened. Only one sentry was now on duty, and no
Frenchmen were to be seen; and he gathered from the idlers,
always to be found hanging about examining posts, that the
latter had been arrested. They had been interrogated, it
appeared, by the sentry with the spectacles. He was evidently
even more intelligent than Carey and I had given him credit
for!

According to the information that our guide brought back,
the Frenchmen had been arrested as a result of their suspicious accent, and had been taken to a guardroom some

distance away from the bridge. Declassé, on hearing this bad news, had lost no time in getting back to us, and it was clear that he was now agitated and nervous, for we immediately left the main road and traipsed across country over difficult and treacherous boggy ground. He was evidently afraid that the Frenchmen would give us away, and that we should be followed and caught before we could reach Antwerp.

At 6.30 we arrived at a fort, or rather I should say a heap of bricks and charred timbers which had once been a fort, part of the outer defences of Antwerp. Twenty minutes later we reached a railway crossing which served as an examining post for all pedestrians entering or leaving the city at that point and, just as we reached it, the gates were closed to let a train through. The result was that, by the time they were opened again, a small crowd had collected on both sides. So the sentries, being hard-pressed, examined no papers properly. It was simply a case of walking on without let or hindrance. We had been lucky again!

A short journey on a tram now brought us to a building over which flew the Red Cross flag.[1] We entered with Declassé. Disappointment followed here. The Belgian in charge informed us that it was being taken over on the morrow by the Germans for the purpose of clearing Belgian refugees, who were now beginning to return from Holland whither they had fled during the siege of the city, but he gave us permission to stay there for the night, and fixed us up with a bed in one of the wash-houses telling us to be sure to clear out early next morning. Before I could get to sleep that night my thoughts went out to those two Frenchmen. Poor devils! I wonder what happened to them.

Early next morning our guide took us away, and installed us in an hotel opposite the Zoological Gardens close to

1. What this building was I do not know, but the International Red Cross should have had nothing to do with escaping soldiers.   *Editor*

the Central Railway Station. It was called the Hôtel
d'Espérance. This very name gave us hope, and in the afternoon Declassé left us assuring us that everything had been
arranged at the hotel, and that there would be nothing for
us to pay. As, however, I had not seen him make these
arrangements, or pay over any cash to the proprietress, and
knowing him as I did, I had my doubts as to whether any
arrangements really had been made. This was Saturday. He
promised to return on Monday to fix up our escape.

I have seen it stated that every man who went through the
hands of Miss Cavell was given money to meet his expenses
and help him get over the frontier. So far as Carey and I
were concerned, this statement was just not true. She never
gave us anything. Nor did we ever get a penny from any other
member of the organisation. Whether of course Declassé was
given money to hand over to us but kept it himself, I cannot
say. I had always doubted the genuineness of Declassé. I had
not long to wait now before my doubts were fully confirmed.
Anyhow that night we did sleep comfortably.

On Sunday morning Carey and I were attracted to the
courtyard outside the Central Station, not more than fifty
yards from our hotel, by the strains of a German military
band playing classical music as only Germans can render it.
The audience consisted of troops and a few civilians, and,
being an ex-bandsman myself, I enjoyed and recognised
many of the pieces that they played. Indeed, I almost
imagined I was back at home in the park, until my eyes came
to rest on the sandbagged entrance to the railway station
with its machine-gun emplacements commanding every
approach. Even the gunners were at their posts, ready to
open fire down the Avenue du Kaiser, or any other approach,
in case of an attack by the civilian population but, as the
German forces appeared to outnumber them by about two
to one, this display of military might struck me as mere

exhibitionism. As for the Flemish themselves, they were freely fraternising with the Germans, and did not seem anything like so antagonistic to the occupation as the Walloons in the south where we had spent most of our time. After the concert we had a meal in the public restaurant of the hotel, where we were forced to mix with German engine drivers and guards off the trains from across the way. So I left it to Carey, with his command of French, to order our food. How we were going to pay for it was another matter.

On Sunday night while having our supper we were confronted by the proprietress. She presented us with a bill for sixty francs, and demanded payment, which, as Carey and I had not five francs between us, was somewhat embarrassing. Further, as there were many Germans in the room, it was obviously inadvisable to start an argument in public. So Carey induced the woman to come with us outside where, on studying the bill, we found that, not only were we being asked to pay for the food that we had eaten ourselves, but also for Declassé's breakfast and dinner of the day before!

There was little doubt that he had failed us. When he found that Red Cross place had been taken over by the Germans he had dumped us in this hotel to get rid of us, without money or friends, and by so doing had placed us in a terrible position. Only after a lengthy argument with the proprietress could we induce her to wait until Monday night for settlement of our account by telling her that we had a friend who had promised to pay for everything on our behalf on his return. We still had a faint hope that Declassé would turn up again. By Monday night however no Declassé had arrived—not that we really expected him—and after a further argument on Tuesday evening she told us that, if our account was not paid by midday on Wednesday, she would call in the police. This she clearly meant to do; and calling in the Antwerp police amounted for us to the same thing as being handed over to the Germans. These Flemish police would not have given us a chance.

The proprietress was obviously in some doubt as to who we were. She knew we were not Belgians. She may have thought that we were Germans. Had she known that we were British soldiers, I am certain that she would have handed us over to the police at once. I am quite sure of that. As it was, having no luggage, we were well watched that Wednesday morning, and saw no hope whatever of leaving the hotel without paying our account. Arrest and the inevitable end now stared us in the face! It was, indeed, a bleak outlook; a bitter fate to contemplate after all our hopes and after all we had gone through. We sat there in blank despair. Then I had a brain wave. It suddenly occurred to me that on my way to the hotel on the Saturday I had seen a building with '*American Commission for Relief in Belgium*' placarded on it.[1] This put a bright idea into my head. I put it to Carey. Americans! People who spoke our own tongue would surely help us, if they knew our plight?

I went and saw the proprietress, and told her that I was just going out to see a friend from whom I knew I could obtain the cash to settle our account, and to my surprise she agreed to this, provided that Carey remained in the hotel as a hostage pending my return. So, with alternate hope and misgiving in my heart, I quickly made my way to this building where on arrival I found my way barred by a commissionaire. He could not speak French, and as there were many Germans in the corridor, some of whom looked

1. In October 1914 the British Government agreed to allow food into Belgium, if it was purchased by the U.S.A., consigned to the American Minister in Brussels, and distributed by him to the civilian population. This led to the American Commission for Relief in Belgium, i.e. C.R.B., under Mr Herbert Clark Hoover, much of the work of which, on the spot, was carried out by young American university graduates.   *Editor*

at me with much suspicion, I dared not try English on him. All I could do now was to return to the hotel and report failure to Carey. Our last hope had gone!

It was now about 11.30 a.m., half an hour to go before we would be arrested! The sand was running out! So Carey decided, as he knew a little Flemish, that he would have a try to find someone on the American Commission. He, too, now saw the proprietress, and informed her that my friend was not at home, but that he had thought of another friend who would gladly pay our account, assuring her that everything would be settled by twelve o'clock as she had requested. Again she agreed to let him go. Money meant more to her than having us arrested!

Before Carey left I asked him not to come back, if he failed, saying that I thought I could make a get-away from the back of the hotel by squeezing myself through a lavatory window. Carey would not hear of this.

'Whatever happens, old pal,' he said, 'I shall come back, and we will see things through together.'

This situation did not arise. Again our luck had held. Five minutes before twelve, zero hour for our arrest, Carey returned, looking jubilant. I knew before he opened his mouth that he had succeeded. He had been luckier than I had been, and related how, when he reached the building, there was no sign of either a commissionaire or of Germans. So he walked straight through the door and down the corridor, without anyone objecting, until he saw a door on which a card was tacked bearing the one word: '*Commissioner*'. Boldly he turned the handle, and walked in. A middle-aged man, who sat writing at a desk, looked up in surprise, and Carey seizing the bull by the horns, asked him in French if he was an American. He was, and Carey explained without delay who he was and our predicament. Could he, please, help us?

The Commissioner listened until Carey had finished his story. Then without hesitation he replied:

'Carey, I believe your story. It rings true. Tell me, what part of Ireland do you come from?'

'Tralee, sor,' said Carey.

'That's strange,' replied the Commissioner. 'My mother was Irish, and she came from Tralee, and for her sake I will do all in my power to help you. Now, tell me what plans you have for the future. Do you wish to stay in Antwerp, or do you want to get back to the old country?'

'Get back to the old country, sor,' replied Carey.

'Right!' said the Commissioner, 'that's the only reply I expected or wanted. Now, listen. Return to your hotel, and in a few minutes I will send a trustworthy Belgian to settle your account. You will be able to recognise him by a bandage round the little finger of his left hand. Immediately he enters, go up and talk to him, just as if you had known him all your life but, above all, never, never come to this building again. All who enter or leave it may be watched. Any communication you wish to make to me in future must be through my representative. You will meet him in a few minutes. It may be many weeks before we get you across into Holland. In the meantime you will be safe here in Antwerp. Do not get impatient if you should have a long wait. There are many hazards in this kind of thing. The wire on the frontier has been strengthened and electrified, and it is very difficult to find a guide who will undertake the dangerous task of negotiating it. Well,' he concluded, grasping Carey by the hand, 'goodbye and good luck, and God be with you.'

Then, handing Carey a box of cigars, he let him out of the door with an encouraging pat on the back. Carey left the building treading on air. Our uncanny luck still held!

The Commissioner was as good as his word. Almost before

Carey had had time to inform the proprietress that his friend would arrive in a few minutes to settle our account, the man with the bandage on the little finger of his left hand walked into the restaurant. Carey approached him, and greeted him as an old friend, and within half an hour the three of us were settled down to lunch in a private room, that mistrusting old lady, the proprietress, now ready to eat out of our hands! Nothing was too good for us. Money talked where she was concerned.

That afternoon our new friend conducted us on a sight-seeing tour of the city. In the evening we accompanied him home to his café in a back street, not more than fifteen minutes' walk from our hotel, and in the course of conversation discovered that he had been a steward on a Belgian-American Red Star liner, which was now laid up owing to the war, and in consequence of which he was out of a regular job. He had an excellent command of English, which he spoke with an American accent. He also seemed a master of bad language. Indeed, he was the most foul-mouthed man that I have ever met and, when upset, could swear for five minutes without using the same word twice! He would never disclose his real name.

'Just call me John,' he said, 'that'll do.'

While out with him next day I met the captain of his ship. He invited us to a café for a drink and, on learning who I was, paid for it with a twenty-mark German note, and pushed his change across the table to me, saying that he hated German money, and advised me to put it in my pocket. He made this a habit, and did the same thing several times on subsequent occasions, gifts which, in addition to the sixteen francs a day I received from the Commissioner, made me a relatively rich man. The captain also lent me a number of English books, and gave me some underclothing and an overcoat in respect of both of which I stood badly in need.

In short, he was a generous man. I was lucky to have met him.

For this and other reasons our long stay in Antwerp was nothing like as tedious as it might have been. During the day Carey preferred to stay in the hotel reading or, maybe, he had some other attraction about which he did not say much! I liked to roam about the city, admiring its fine buildings, the cathedral, the Hôtel de Ville, and the Steen. There was also a fine promenade along the quay to which I often went. And I had much to interest and amuse me; the shops of the diamond dealers and watching them sorting out and weighing their diamonds, and haggling over prices—traffic in these still went on in spite of the war—and the fat German soldiers performing their ridiculous goose-step whenever they passed an officer. The cinemas and theatres were also in full swing. There was no charge for admission to the former but once inside you were expected to buy a drink. The interiors were laid out on the café principle, chairs round small tables, and as soon as one was seated a waiter appeared and asked for your order. I always called for *café Russe*, not because I was fond of it, but because I could pronounce that without fear of complications.

One afternoon I visited one of these cinemas, and had just got comfortably seated when a German N.C.O. came in and sat down opposite me at the same table. It was clear to me that he wanted to talk and, short of getting to my feet and walking out, I saw no way of avoiding it. (In those days all films were silent, and it was the custom to visit a cinema for a chat and a drink while watching one.) Nervously I waited for him to begin, which he did by enquiring if I could speak French? Whereupon I asked him if he could speak Flemish? He said, 'No.' So I then told him I spoke Flemish, and just a little French. This pleased him. He had met someone on whom he could practise his French, which he was learning

M

in anticipation of getting a good post in the Civil Administration when Germany took Belgium over after the war. This, he said, could not last for many more weeks! I now discovered that my French was superior to his, and felt fairly safe in asking a few questions, such as the number of Germans in Antwerp. Before parting he stood me a drink—the second I had got at German expense—and said that he had enjoyed my company, and hoped to meet me again. In case he was smarter than he appeared, however, I deliberately failed to keep the appointment which we made.

When I got separated from Heath on the day of the scare at the clinic in Brussels, I also got separated from my shaving gear. We only had one razor between us! This awkward situation meant that I had to go to a barber every other day, and I would hover round his shop until it was empty of customers, and then dash in and, throwing myself into a chair, exclaim, '*Razez moi vite.*' And it did not matter how much the barber talked. (Those Belgian barbers were no exception to the English rule.) He got no conversation out of me. Then I paid with a one-franc note, waited for my change, and got out of his shop as quickly as I could. I also made a rule never to patronise the same man twice. By the time we left Antwerp I had great difficulty in finding a barber who had not shaved me before!

Almost every evening Carey and I forgathered at the café where our mysterious friend, whom we had been told to call John, lived. We managed to have a lot of fun there. Whether he was the proprietor of it or not we never quite discovered. Anyhow German soldiers sometimes came in for a drink. They irritated him beyond words, and he would abuse them from behind the counter in English with the finest flow of language that it has ever been my privilege to listen to. These Germans, of course, did not understand one word, and thought he was paying them compliments, and some-

times invited him to have one on them, offers which, for
some reason, he always refused. I could never quite understand why. Many of these incidents were highly entertaining
for us spectators in the know, but they might have had
awkward consequences if one of those Germans had understood the meaning of the words he used.

13

Holland at last!

On may 16th we were advised by our friend that the Commissioner had made arrangements for us to be guided across the frontier the following night. This seemed, after all the time we had been waiting, almost too good to be true, and that evening we were introduced to the man who was to take us over; a wizened old chap, almost a dwarf, and some sixty years of age. He certainly did not inspire confidence. As he could only speak Flemish, we could only ask him questions through John, and his replies to these, we thought, were evasive. So we came away with a poor opinion of the man who was to pilot us on the most desperate part of our venture. There was nothing we could do about it however. We were forced to accept him now, hoping that his appearance would prove to have been deceptive.

Anyhow, on the following evening, we said goodbye to the proprietress and the staff at the hotel where we had been staying. The dear lady now apologised for her behaviour at the beginning of our stay, and said she was really sorry that we were leaving, being, of course, still completely ignorant as to who we really were. We then went to John's café where we found a farewell supper provided for us, and champagne, too, in honour of the occasion. We would need it, he said. It was a good twelve miles from the northern outskirts of Antwerp to the frontier, and in order to reach it, we would have to dodge two lines of sentries and evade many parties of Germans patrolling the wire. A formidable and dangerous adventure clearly lay ahead of us. He also gave both Carey and myself a peculiar-shaped pearl button.

'These,' he said, 'are to be given to your guide when he hands you over to the Belgian Consul at Roosendaal.'

He also told us to ask the Belgian Consul to make quite sure that our guide understood that these buttons were to be returned to him as proof that we had actually got through. He would then be entitled to receive payment for the job he had done. This, I believe, was to be three pounds for each of us, only, of course, if we got through.

At about 8.30 p.m. John, as we called him, accompanied us, travelling by tram, to the northern outskirts of the city. There he said goodbye, and wished us all luck. Neither the American Commissioner nor he himself, he said, would be happy until those pearl buttons were sewn on the former's waistcoat again from which they had been taken. Those two had been good friends to us indeed!

It must have been about 9 p.m. when we started for that 'strip' about which we had already heard so much. The night was ideal for the venture; raining heavily, blowing hard, and visibility a bare few feet ahead. Our guide soon proved marvellous, and we quickly gained confidence in him. Old though he was, Carey and I had great difficulty in keeping pace with him in the dark. He could see like a cat. Further, he had no respect for property. He took us through the gates of houses and across lawns and gardens without any hesitation. We waded ditches with the water up to his waist. Eventually, after about three hours, having crossed and re-crossed a railway several times, we emerged from a copse near a derelict cottage at the barbed wire itself. Only a few hundred yards away we could see the brightly lit Dutch frontier!

For some time we stood there listening. All we heard was

the wind, and the clocks in Holland striking midnight. The blood was racing through our veins. We were in a fever pitch of excitement. But between us and liberty there still extended a formidable barbed-wire entanglement, reported to be electrified in places, and, in the dark, we could not even see the other side. Beyond it lay five hundred yards of neutral ground. Then Holland! Could we make it?

Our guide motioned to us to lie down, and left us for about ten minutes. Then he returned and, stripping off all his clothes, except his boots, indicated to us that we were to do the same.[1]

Carey, not understanding his motive, whispered to me:

'Surely he doesn't expect us to go into Holland naked?'

'That will do me,' I replied, 'if I can get there.'

Carey's fears were soon dispelled. The little old man produced three lengths of cord. Then, giving each of us one, he proceeded to tie his own clothes into a bundle with the third, and having done this, flung it over the wire to the other side. My length of rope was rather short, and insufficient to tie up my clothes if I included my overcoat. So I left it out, and when I tried to throw it over after my bundle, it got caught in the wind and landed somewhere on top of the wire. There it had to stay as a present for the Germans. (I had left nothing of value in any of its pockets.) Then the three of us, all stark naked except for our boots, and with our bundles somewhere the other side, each selected a spot where the wire seemed most flexible, i.e. somewhere about half-way between the posts that held it, and started to worm our way through. Wriggling forward on our stomachs a few inches at

1. This method may surprise some but anyone with experience of negotiating ordinary barbed-wire fences will realise that this was the only way to get through, particularly in the dark. Clothing has no sensory nerves like skin and catches without warning. In clothes they would have got stuck. Naked, they could feel their way through. Besides, skin tears. Clothing often will not.   *Editor*

a time, then retreating a little as a barb impaled itself in our flesh, with terror in our hearts lest the creak of the wire (the sound of which was no doubt amplified for us by the tension of the moment and the silence of the night) would bring along a patrol, our progress seemed painfully slow. And it was slow! For the entanglement had been constructed with characteristic German thoroughness. It was an iron wire cobweb at least thirty feet in depth! But, after what seemed like an hour, although I suppose it was probably really not more than fifteen minutes, we all three emerged panting on the other side. We were through! Liberty was in sight!

For a little while we lay there naked on the damp earth, exhausted by our efforts, soaked by the rain, and with our backs smarting with pain and bleeding from the scratches and lacerations we had received. But we lay there only long enough to recover our strength and breath for the final dash across neutral ground to Holland and to freedom. How can one describe one's thoughts as we listened for Germans? But no sounds, other than those made by the wind and the rain, came from the side of the wire we had left. Perhaps the patrols were sheltering from the dirty weather. If so, who could blame them?

Then, feeling we had recovered sufficiently for the last lap of all, with one accord we each grabbed a bundle of clothing, irrespective of to whom it really belonged, and commenced crawling towards those alluring lights now not so very far away. We crawled about fifty yards. Then our guide grunted something, and jumped to his feet. This was the signal for the final dash. And dash we did! I had not dashed far, however, before I plunged headlong into a deep ditch full of water, bundle and all, this sudden immersion taking all my breath away, but in a few seconds I had retrieved my bundle, scrambled out, and was not far behind my companions by the time we reached the wire on the Dutch side. This con-

sisted of two strands each about three feet high. We stepped
elegantly over it, waded another dyke, and walked across a
cottage garden, and then through a gate straight into the
arms of a Dutch guard.

He and our guide seemed to be old friends, and chatted
away gaily while we dressed. Then we shook hands with our
Dutch friend, who gave each of us a round of ammunition
as a souvenir, and patted us on the back, saying, '*Goot
Engleesh*'. All danger was over now. There were no more
risks to be run, and we set off down the road at a jaunty
pace to try and warm ourselves up. After about an hour's
going we arrived at a quaint Dutch inn. There our guide
roused the innkeeper and his wife. He appeared to know
them well, and at about 2 a.m. or thereabouts we sat down
to bread, cheese, pickles, and Dutch beer. Then, the keeper
of the inn having supplied us with blankets and taken away
our sodden clothes, we wrapped ourselves up and were soon
fast asleep on the sanded floor, dreaming of Home.

We slept until roused at about 8 a.m. by our host, who now
returned us our clothing, still dirty, but more or less dry! And
our guide somehow succeeded in making us understand that
it was fourteen miles to Roosendaal. We could walk, or ride
if we could afford to pay for it, he said. So, now relatively
wealthy, and thinking that we had done more than enough
walking during the past few weeks, we opted for a conveyance of some kind regardless of expense. We did not have to
wait long. Soon, seated in a smart dog-cart behind a snappy
little pony, we were rattling gaily down the road in the bright
morning sunshine through the woods of Holland. The trees
were just bursting into leaf. That ride to Roosendaal will
ever stick in my memory!

Soon after we arrived we were closeted with the Belgian
Consul through whom our guide now received from us those
two pearl buttons worth three pounds each to him. Then,

bidding us goodbye in Flemish, he left us. He had certainly proved himself a wonderful old man. He must have known every inch of the country from Antwerp to the frontier, or he could never have brought us through in the dark without ever even hearing a German sentry. The Consul told us that he knew him very well. He had crossed the frontier both ways at least once a week for the last three or four months. This was the first time that he had brought anyone over it with him however. Hitherto he had only carried letters. The Consul also told us that we were far from being the first British soldiers to pass through his hands, and said that we could not be interned. We had not entered Holland in uniform. Very kindly, too, he enquired if we had any money? So, remembering that I had no pay for nine months, and being somewhat doubtful if I was really entitled to any, and thinking that whatever I might be able to get from him would be a fair charge on the British Government, who I did think did owe me something, I said 'No' emphatically, before Carey could possibly answer 'Yes'. Whereupon he gave us three guilders each, and a piece of paper on which was written the address of the British Consul in Flushing.

We arrived there early that evening, and within ten minutes were relating our experiences to the Consul himself who, while he was preparing our passports, told us that he would send us to Rotterdam next day. We should be able to get a boat from there much sooner, he said, and, like the Belgian consul at Roosendaal, wanted to know if we wanted any money. Carey got in first this time with a definite 'Yes, sor'. Then he sent us to an hotel on the sea front for the night.

In the hectic days that followed my departure from the clinic in Brussels, I had almost forgotten, I am ashamed to say, my old comrade Heath, but while signing my name in the hotel register that night I spotted a signature among those of previous arrivals which was undoubtedly his. So I made enquiries of the porter, and learnt that a man, who from his description almost certainly was Heath, had left for Rotterdam only two days before. The old spark had beaten me on the post after all, and I was thankful to know that he, too, had got safely through. I now hoped to catch up with him at Rotterdam where, I was told, six British soldiers, who had recently crossed the frontier at various points, were still waiting for a boat. I did! As I came into the room for breakfast next morning, there sat Heath! The surprise was, of course, his, for I knew that I was following on his heels. It was good to think, we agreed, that, after all we had gone through together, we were reunited for the last and final stage of our long journey home.[1]

At 10 a.m. we were all interviewed individually by the British Consul at Rotterdam, a fatherly old chap, who gave us five shillings each without even asking if we wanted it! Then, handing us our tickets for the boat, he instructed us to board the S.S. *Copenhagen* as soon as it was dark.

'After you get on board,' he said, 'you will probably be questioned by the Dutch Immigration Authorities. Just tell them that you are travellers for a British firm of tile manufacturers and building materials. That's the password. Don't forget.'

The boat was crowded with Belgian refugees, mostly women. Late that evening we slipped out of Rotterdam without lights, and after supper we six soldiers forgathered on the upper deck, where we remained swopping experiences until everyone else had long since gone to bed. Then one by one my comrades also disappeared, until I was left alone, content to remain leaning over the ship's side, watching her

---

1. I asked Beaumont how Heath got across the frontier. He did it, apparently, by the classical method, and never had to worm naked through the wire. He got through hidden under the hay in a haycart travelling by one of the roads!   *Editor*

plough her way towards England through a calm sea in the blackness of the night, and thinking. My thoughts were not the ordinary ones of a soldier coming home. I had been missing for nine months. Had my wife been able to find out what had happened to me? It was most unlikely. Probably I had been reported killed. Then thoughts of this kind were interrupted by one of the stewards who joined me, and did his best to make me nervous with his tales of German submarines. They were very active in this vicinity, he said. I refused to be scared. My experiences in Belgium had long since steeled my nerves. At last I, too, decided to turn in.

When I woke up the ship was riding quietly at anchor at the mouth of the Thames waiting for a pilot and the tide to take us up the river.

Early in the afternoon we berthed at Tilbury, and we soldiers were taken off by a Customs cutter and handed over to the G.O.C. Thames Defences at Gravesend who, on learning who we were and whence we had come, got in touch with the War Office and was told to detain us 'pending further instructions'. In the meantime we were forbidden to communicate with anyone outside the fort, a restriction which seemed to me unreasonable.

The following day we were interviewed by an officer from the Intelligence Branch of the War Office. He questioned us on anything we might have seen while in occupied territory, and our replies were taken down in shorthand. I told him of the airships I had seen at Evere. He thanked me for this, and said that this information might be very valuable, but warned me at the same time that I was bound by the Official Secrets Act and must not tell anyone else what I had told him. Six weeks later those airships were destroyed, I heard, in their hangars by two seaplanes of the Royal Naval Air Service, and the shots fired by the German anti-aircraft guns to beat off this attack were, I believe, the only shots fired over Brussels during the whole war. Whether this was the direct result of the information I had brought home, of course, I do not know.

In the afternoon we were all sent off to our respective regiments, and our arrival at the Royal West Kent Depot at Maidstone did create something of a stir. Since that day, I regret to say, I have neither heard nor seen anything of Carey. But I kept up with Heath. He had been reported as wounded and missing, presumably a prisoner of war. I had been reported, as I feared, killed in action on August 24th, 1914, and had accordingly been struck off the strength of the regiment. Further, I was told that I could not be taken on it again until some officer or N.C.O., the latter not below the rank of sergeant, could identify me. So, as nobody at the depot knew me, things appeared rather awkward, until I suggested that they check up the tattoo mark of mine against my medical record. That settled it! The Union Jack on my arm left no doubt in the official mind that I was after all the man I had claimed to be!

Nevertheless, we were virtually under open arrest for the time being, confined to barracks and still forbidden to communicate with anyone outside the depot. The following morning we paraded before the commandant. He informed us that we were under orders to remain there 'at the disposal of the War Office', and he demanded a report of our nine months' 'absence without leave', and seemed quite disappointed to learn that we had already rendered our reports to the War Office. We had been firmly instructed not to report to anyone else.

'Very well!' he said. 'Meet me and the other officers of the depot in the mess this afternoon, and tell us of your escapade. What you say will be regarded as confidential by all those present.'

So for two hours that afternoon Heath and I, comfortably

installed in the best armchairs in the officers' mess, related our adventures to our C.O. and his brother officers, and at the end of our story the Colonel was so impressed that he telephoned the War Office for permission to send us home on leave. This was not granted, but they did at least agree that our next of kin should be notified of our return at long last, and be allowed to come and see us. So, within minutes, telegrams were on their way to our wives and mothers, notifying them of our continued existence in this world, and inviting them to come to Maidstone at once with all expenses paid, the last sentence being added by the Colonel, who paid all my wife's expenses out of his own pocket.

I have often wondered what my wife's feelings must have been when she got that telegram, and next day she told me that there had been doubt in her mind about my death at first. Captain Taylor had reported my whereabouts, when he succeeded in regaining the British lines in France, and Maurice Demoustier, when he arrived in England, had got in touch with the manager of Heath's firm who communicated the facts to the War Office. They passed them on to my wife. But, after six months, as there was no trace of me in the returns of prisoners of war received from Germany through the Red Cross, I was written off as dead, my wife informed accordingly, and arrangements made for her to draw her widow's pension. So far as the War Office was concerned I was dead, and only my appearance in person could alter that decision. I do not think that my wife had ever quite believed them.

Early in August that year our commanding officer received a telegram from the War Office, instructing us to proceed to the White City to identify a Belgian refugee, who claimed to have suffered at the hands of the Germans as a result of sheltering us in his house. On arrival there we found Neusy, his wife and his son! After Marie had served her month's imprisonment, they told us, the Germans played hell with them. Again and again they descended on their house, searched it (but never found that rifle), smashed their furniture in doing it and were just as rough with it and them as they damned well could be. Eventually their only course was to get out.

Then we were instructed to accompany Neusy to the War Office, and here we endorsed his qualifications as a great patriot. Shortly after he was taken on by the British secret service. He would never tell us in exactly what capacity. He could be as close as an oyster when he chose. But he was just the man for the job. The more dangerous it was, the better would M. Neusy like it![1]

---

1. Neusy was handsomely compensated by the British Government for the damage to his house and effects, and for the personal service he had rendered to Heath and myself. His wife Marie, Mmme Demoustier, and Marie Godart were presented with medals and received letters of thanks both from the British and Belgian Governments.   *Author*

Epilogue[1]

HARRY BEAUMONT wormed his naked body through the wire and crossed the frontier into neutral Holland on May 18th. In occupied Belgium the axe fell on July 31st. For the Germans had grown increasingly suspicious, and their secret police correspondingly vigilant, although they continued to play cat and mouse with many members of the organisation, notably with Miss Cavell and her circle in Brussels, until they had accumulated sufficient evidence on which to act in respect of them all.

Philippe Baucq, the Belgian architect, and Louise Thuliez, the French schoolmistress, were arrested first, late that night at the former's house in Brussels. Ada Bodart's son, a schoolboy, and a friend of his Constant Cayron, a student, were arrested next day. Miss Cavell was arrested a few days later in her nursing school, and Capiau, Libiez, Ada Bodart, the Countess Jean de Belleville, and the Princess Marie de Croy very soon after. Many humble people were also arrested, both in the Borinage and in the neighbourhood of Bellignies, round about this time. Only Prince Réginald managed to escape at the last moment, after many adventures, an account of which is given in the Appendix to this book, by kind permission of his sister, the Princess Marie de Croy.

Most of those arrested, certainly all the important ones, were now relegated to solitary confinement in the prison of St Gille in Uccle, a suburb to the south of Brussels. Here

1. This is based on the last chapter of Beaumont's MSS., conversation with him, and facts gleaned from other sources.   *Editor*

they were subjected to repeated interrogation by the police, and many tricked into candid confession as to everything they had done. Mlle Thuliez and Miss Cavell both fell into this trap, the latter admitting, as she did again at her trial later, that she had helped two hundred British and Belgians, in one way or another, to get away from Brussels. Only the Princess Marie de Croy, it seems, and Philippe Baucq, the architect, both more wordly wise, obstinately refused.

Six weeks later all those who had been arrested were arraigned before a military court sitting in the Parliament House in Brussels. Admittedly their trial was a rushed and scrambled affair, all these thirty-five accused persons being tried by a panel of seven judges in the brief space of two days. Nevertheless, they were defended by counsel, and no legal right was actually denied them. Further, they had offended against the regulations promulgated by the Germans, legally under International Law, to ensure the safety of their armed forces in occupied Belgium. No serious exception can in fact be taken to their trial.[1]

Judgement was passed on the third day by the Court sitting in secret session. Five of the accused, two men and three women, namely, Philippe Baucq and Louis Séverin who had sheltered Beaumont for a while, and the Countess Jeanne de Belleville, Mlle Thuliez, and Miss Cavell who had also sheltered him, were condemned to death for 'war treason' against the German State in that they had 'conveyed recruits to the enemy'. Herman Capiau, who had helped Beaumont so much and figures prominently in his narrative, Capiau's friend and collaborator, Albert Libiez, Ada Bodart, the Irish widow, and Georges Derveau, were sentenced to fifteen years' hard labour for the same offence.

1. I have discussed the legality under International Law of the German position in Belgium in 1914 and that of the trial in my book on Edith Cavell.   *Editor*

The Princess Marie de Croy was sentenced to ten, and several others, including Beaumont's friend, Demoustier, to periods of hard labour ranging from two to eight years. Eight alone of the thirty-five were actually acquitted.

Two days later the sentences were confirmed by General von Saubersweig, the newly appointed Military Governor of Brussels, and the prisoners were assembled in the hall of the prison to hear them read. Their sentences could now be executed, and von Saubersweig, determined to make an example of someone and stop underground activity, and possessed by a passionate hatred of England, deliberately hurried on the execution of Baucq and Cavell before the sentences were made public, in order to avoid any possible appeal for mercy on their behalf from outside. The sentence on Miss Cavell leaked out however, and a desperate effort was made by the American Legation to save her at the last moment. But von Saubersweig was adamant; her execution was 'absolutely necessary to ensure the safety of German troops in Brussels'. This was nonsense, of course; and he may well have been under the influence of drink when he rejected the American appeal. Nevertheless, in so doing, drunk or sober, he was still acting within his legal right under German military law as it stood then. So Baucq and Cavell paid the supreme penalty for their patriotism in defying it at the hands of the same firing party at dawn on October 12th, 1915.[1]

Whether any members of the organisation, other than Prince Réginald, escaped, we do not know for certain. Nor do we know how many active members of it, of whom the world has never heard, were never seriously suspected and

1. A statue depicting the execution of Baucq was put up in Brussels after the war but when during the Second World War the British radio appealed to Belgians to emulate him, and join the resistance movement, the Germans thought it advisable to blow it up. A new one is about to be erected.   *Editor*

now went underground. There may have been many in this category. Nor do we know how many Belgians befriended British fugitives *without* actively helping them to escape, or helped their friends to befriend them. A very large number certainly did, and many took great risks in doing it, Beaumont's story revealing the work and names of some at least of these hitherto unrecognised and unsung patriots. The Neusys, for example, and Marie and Grandma Godart, and Leon Philliperon who gave Beaumont that life-saving dictionary, and the postmaster at Wasmes, never came under suspicion, or anyhow never came under it sufficiently to be arrested by the Germans. Nor did the axe ever fall, as far as I know, on the monastery at Averbode. Nor, again as far as I know, was any priest or nun or monk, although many were active in helping and nursing fugitives, ever arrested for that offence. Perhaps even the Germans, who had been fools enough to shoot Miss Cavell, realised that this would have been politically unwise.

One man, who could have got away, refused the opportunity to go and so, under military law, became a deserter from the Army. His is a tragic story; a Munster Fusilier, befriended by, and found living with, a French woman in the Mormal district. At length he was persuaded to leave her, and was guided into Brussels with a party of other fugitives *en route* for the Dutch frontier. There he was hidden in Miss Cavell's clinic but, while he was there, he deliberately escaped to return to the woman with whom he had become entangled. This naturally caused the organisation grave anxiety. He could have given away so much to the Germans. This part of the story is confirmed by Louise Thuliez in her *Condemned to Death* (page 52, see footnote on page 21). The sequel to it is related by Beaumont, who got it from Capiau after the war was over. Dr B., the English doctor who visited the soldiers in Miss Cavell's clinic, and dealt peremptorily with the Irishman (but about whom I have been unable to discover anything), realising that a dangerous security risk was now at large, sent a message to Capiau to the effect that this man was probably returning to Mormal via Wasmes. He also urged him to intercept and kill him, and Beaumont says that Capiau actually intended to do this (which under the circumstances might have been justified in civil law), so great did he think the risk of him giving the secrets of the organisation away to the Germans, which might have led to the death of many members of it. Capiau failed to intercept him, however, and never saw or heard of the man again until one day in 1916 when he himself was in prison in Germany, he was suddenly summoned to the Governor's office to interpret for a British fugitive who had just been arrested and brought in. This proved to be the Munster Fusilier. Capiau now did his best for him, but he never learned his fate. He had escaped being shot as a deserter by the British and by the organisation for letting them down. Whether he escaped being shot as a spy by the Germans history does not relate.

Apart from the tragic case of this one man, all British fugitives helped by the organisation to escape—a few refused their help—with the single exception of Colonel Bodger (see page 19), apparently got away. How many men the organisation actually helped to get away is, however, not definitely known. The Germans put the figure at 250. Miss Cavell at her trial said she helped about 200 in some way or another, but some of these were French and some Belgian, and all British fugitives did not pass through her hands. The German figure is probably not far out, and of these about 150–200 were probably British.

This was a notable achievement for which the organisation had now paid in blood and, to quote Churchill's words spoken in another war, were now destined to pay in toil and sweat and tears. They had paid for it in blood in the execution of Cavell and Baucq; also in the suicide of Louis Pansaers who took his own life in St Gilles while awaiting his sentence after the trial. (The irony of this tragedy is that in the German view he was only one of the minor offenders, and was, in point of fact, acquitted.) The organisation was destined to pay in toil and sweat in the sentences of hard labour that the others served until the armistice released them. They were destined to pay in tears in that these remained prisoners in a foreign land, ignorant of what had happened to their relatives, fearing the reprisals that might have descended on their homes, haunted by the fear that the Allies might never win the war. And two never did come home: Constant Cayron, the student, and Paul Godefroy, a jeweller, both dying in captivity.

After the Cavell tragedy escaping still continued. Most fugitive soldiers who had evaded capture had now probably got away,[1] anyhow few escaped after that, but Belgians and French of military age and technicians useful to the Allies went on getting out of the country, often across the frontier

---

1. Not all had. The Marquis of Cambridge, who was in the advance on Mons in 1918, tells me how they came across two Cameron High-landers who had been living disguised as civilians ever since the retreat in 1914. He also directed my attention to the remarkable story of Trooper Patrick Fowler of the 11th Hussars, published in the *Cavalry Journal* of July 1927 (Vol. XVII, p. 445), who was concealed by Mme and Mlle Belmont-Gobert in a wardrobe in her cottage close behind the German lines, and in a room which was sometimes occupied by German soldiers, with the connivance of their neighbour, in spite of the terrible risk they were all running the whole time, until released by the Allied advance in October 1918. The same author also tells the tale of Corporal Hull of the same regiment who was concealed in a small room under their roof by M. and Mme Gustave Cardon. Unfortunately, after a year, the Germans got wind of him and he was arrested and shot. Mme Cardon was condemned to hard labour, but her husband escaped, and remained a fugitive in his own country until the war was over. These gallant people were all rewarded by the gift of annuities purchased out of a fund raised by the *Daily Telegraph* at the end of the war.

further east. There it was much less strictly guarded. The Neusys arrived in England in 1916,[1] and a Dr Bull, an elderly man and dental surgeon to King Albert (who may have been the mysterious Dr B. who visited the soldiers in Miss Cavell's clinic), was arrested in 1916, and sentenced to three months' imprisonment and to pay a heavy fine for 'helping Prisoners and young Belgians to escape'.[2] Whether the Commissioner in Antwerp who helped Beaumont and Carey to get away, and whose name we do not know, also helped others to do it we do not know either. On the whole this seems unlikely. In doing what he did to help Beaumont and Carey he had already risked his own position. If he had gone on he would have been risking the whole status of the American Organisation for Relief in Belgium which, after all, was only allowed to operate there by permission of the German Government.

Meanwhile the war dragged on. The fighting on the Western Front swayed backwards and forwards in the mud. Neither side broke through, the Allied line held, and in 1917 the Germans, confronted by stalemate, launched unrestricted U-boat warfare against all shipping on the high seas. This brought the United States into the war. Then in March 1918, before the Americans could make any effective contribution in France, Ludendorff launched his great offensive, his objective the Channel ports. Again it was touch and go, and Haigh issued his famous order of the day: 'Each man must fight on to the end.' Again the line held, and although it hardly looked like it at the time, this was really the beginning of the end. The German High Command had shot their bolt and lost, and in July the great Allied advance began.

1. I asked Beaumont how the Neusys got across the frontier into Holland but he could not remember.   *Editor*
2. Brand Whitlock, *Belgium under German Occupation* (Heinemann), London, 1919.

Steadily the Hindenburg Line was overrun, and by the beginning of November the long weary war was drawing to its close at last. Then at the eleventh hour of the eleventh day of the eleventh month on the Western Front the bugles sounded the cease fire and the church bells rang out the Armistice. In London the maroons went off. Everyone rushed out into the street.

In Germany the revolutionaries threw open the prison doors and the political prisoners walked out. Two had died. But all the rest got home. Capiau and Libiez got home. Both died several years ago. Ada Bodart got home. She too is dead. (I have been privileged to meet and talk to her daughter who helped her mother to hide and feed the soldiers in their house.) Louise Thuliez died a short while ago. The Princess Marie de Croy got back to Brussels in time to witness the triumphant return of King Albert to his capital, and in spite of severe illness while in captivity, lived to 'fight again'. For, during the Second World War, she was again overrun at Bellignies by the Germans and again helped British fugitives (airmen who had crash landed) to escape. Again she was arrested, and again put in prison, but this time was released, on grounds of ill-health. She is still alive and, in her ninety-first year, entertained me, and with all her faculties intact told me of it all.

Beaumont had suffered severely as the result of the physical and mental strain of his long nine months as a fugitive. He was not sent abroad again, and was transferred to the Ordnance Corps. Gradually for him, as for so many others, the memory of Mons, and for him those nightmare months as a haunted hunted fugitive, receded. Indeed, it was his Belgian friends, and also, as for so many others, the cama-raderie engendered by the war that he liked to remember. And in 1920 the post one morning brought him a sudden reminder of those days:

WAR OF 1914–1920

7555 Pte. H. W. Beaumont, 1st Bn. R.W.Kent R. was mentioned in the London Gazette for gallant conduct displayed in escaping or attempting to escape from captivity. I have it in command from the King to record His Majesty's high appreciation of the services rendered.

War Office
Whitehall, S.W.
31st July 1920

WINSTON S. CHURCHILL
Secretary of State for War

Heath died a few years ago. Beaumont lives on quietly, content in that he has served his country as a soldier in time of her great need, and also that, as a soldier, he had done his duty in escaping; and happy, too, in that his book, with its tribute to his many friends who helped him, is at long last, after all, to see the light of day!

Appendix

The Escape Organisation in the Etapen[1]

IN ORDER to complete the picture of the escape organisation as a whole, and to do justice to and put into right per-
spective the work of the many patriots who helped fugitive
Allied soldiers to get away, a slightly more detailed account
is required of the part played by the de Croys and Mlles
Thuliez and Moriamé in occupied France *before* they linked
up, through Miss Cavell and her circle in Brussels, with the
work of Capiau and others in the Belgian Borinage. That
which follows is based on the Princess Marie de Croy's *War
Memories* (MacMillan, 1932) and Mlle Thuliez's *Condemned to
Death* (Methuen, 1934), and also on what they told me in the
course of conversation.

Just south of the Franco-Belgian border, the reader will
remember, stood the Château of Bellignies, of various dates,
built round a medieval tower, where, although of Belgian
nationality, lived Prince Leopold de Croy, his brother the
Prince Réginald, and his unmarried sister, the Princess
Marie. When the war started Prince Leopold left to join the
Army, and the Princess, who had trained in Paris as a nurse,
immediately offered the château as a hospital for the wounded to the French Government. Events moved rapidly. On
August 21st came the news that British troops would be
billeted there, and a company of the Middlesex Regiment

1. The part of France occupied by the Germans and under military
law.

arrived that night. Next day General French passed through. Then the retreat began, and British and German wounded were brought in. Soon German advance troops arrived. Then Von Kluck, in command of the army corps on the German right, made it his headquarters. His stay was brief. The German advance swept on, and the château became a Red Cross hospital again.

Before long many more wounded picked up in the neighbourhood, both British and German, were brought in, but after about a fortnight all were transferred to German military hospitals, and peace of a kind reigned at the château again. 'Then one day soon after this, when we were walking round the lawn,' writes the Princess of September 29th, 'two young women standing near the gate asked to speak to Réginald. They were from St Waast, two miles away. One was Mlle Moriamé, the brewer's sister, the other Mlle Louise Thuliez, a schoolmistress from Lille who had been spending her holidays in the village. They wanted to know what they should do with several English soldiers they had nursed for slight wounds, and kept hidden ever since, as notices were now posted everywhere ordering all inhabitants to declare at once any Allied soldiers they had found behind the lines. The penalty for disobedience was death! So, as we still all hoped to see our armies driving the enemy back within a few weeks, we told them to keep them quiet, give out to the village that they had run away, and in the meanwhile Réginald promised to find a safe hiding-place for them.'

At this point Mlle Thuliez tells her own story. 'That very evening,' she writes, 'he [the Prince] directed us to a house at Obies, eight kilometres away, standing in a clearing in the northern part of the forest of Mormal, and we spent the next day collecting civilian clothing for our wounded so that they could get away unnoticed. In the evening we left with them. It was an ideal hiding-place—an English soldier had already been there over a month—as the house had several exits, and they could sleep on the hay in the loft over the cart-shed. Then, leaving them in the care of the people of Obies, we returned to St Waast, and told the Mayor that the Englishmen had insisted on going away, that we had been unable to stop them, and that we did not know in which direction they had gone.'

The problem now was to get these men back to their units when no one knew exactly where the British were or what was happening. So these two young women set off on foot to find the fighting line. They did not find it—it was much too far away—but they did find many other Allied soldiers scattered about the countryside in hiding, among them a party of about forty British soldiers, drawn from various units, and now under the command of Lieutenant Bushell of the 2nd Dragoon Guards (The Queen's Bays). They had constructed a dug-out in which they could conceal themselves when necessary, and had put out sentries, and were being supplied with food by the neighbouring villagers. The Princess herself paid them a visit—in a donkey cart so as not to attract suspicion. But the Germans got wind of them, and their position became precarious. So one night Mlles Moriamé and Thuliez guided them through the forest to join the other fugitives at Obies, and later, when this hideout also became unsafe, through the forest, again under cover of darkness, to the château at Bellignies. There a British officer named Preston, who had escaped from the hospital at Bavay when it was taken over by the Germans, as Beaumont did at Wasmes, was being hidden by the de Croys. Whenever any German came along he withdrew into a secret staircase in the tower.

At Bellignies it was not yet realised that it might be possible to escape and get back to England via neutral Holland. No one was allowed to cross the Franco-Belgian

border without a permit from the German authorities. This
added to the general ignorance prevailing. So, as there
seemed no way of escape, these men eventually agreed
reluctantly to give themselves up rather than continue to
risk the lives of the two young women and the de Croys who
had befriended them. Further, it was becoming difficult to
feed them. They only agreed on the understanding that
every effort would be made to help their two officers to
escape when the opportunity arose.

Giving themselves up was not easy without bringing the
château under suspicion. Further, some of them had thrown
away their uniforms and were disguised as civilians. This
meant that, if they fell into German hands, they would
almost certainly be shot. By collecting uniforms from various
sources, however, they were soon made soldiers again, and
then were guided under cover of night into Bavay, by the two
young women, and handed over to the Mayor who, on learning the situation, reluctantly agreed to hand them over
through the French Red Cross to the German authorities.
They looked in too good shape to have been hiding in a forest
for weeks, and the Germans were highly suspicious of them,
but the château escaped serious suspicion for the time being
and Preston and Bushell remained in hiding there.

In November news reached them through a near neighbour of the de Croys, the Countess Jeanne de Belleville, a
French lady who lived at Montigny-sur-Roc, just north of
the Franco-Belgian frontier, that a certain Miss Cavell,
matron of a clinic in Brussels, had helped Colonel Bodger
and Sergeant Meachin of the Cheshires to get away. The
Countess could easily get into Brussels, and had found a
Belgian priest, the Abbé de Longueville, who undertook to
get her nephew—he was terribly anxious to join the French
Army—across the frontier into neutral Holland. So Preston
and Bushell implored her to help them to escape too.

'At last, a few days after Christmas,' writes the Princess, 'we were able to send our two officers off dressed like well-to-do artisans.' They were guided as far as Mons by Mlle Thuliez and Martha, the latter a faithful servant of the de Croys. There they were met by the Prince who provided them with forged identity cards to get them into Brussels, the forms for which he had got from the *Bureau de Population* in Mons during the lunch-hour when the German in charge was out and his Belgian clerk was free to do what he liked. From Mons they travelled by tram to Brussels. There they were hidden by a M. van der Straten. Thence, dressed as carpenters and carrying their tools, they were guided across the frontier by smugglers. The Abbé was never able to return. His activities had been discovered, and the Germans set a high price on his head.

'Having succeeded so well with the officers,' continues the Princess, 'we were naturally anxious to find any more soldiers concealed behind the lines and get them away too. So Réginald and Jeanne de Belleville, and Mlles Moriamé and Thuliez, toured the neighbourhood every day, bringing in men to rest before they started on their journey.' The two young women particularly tramped miles and miles through the forest, looking for men, and guided them to the château in the dark, often being compelled to make long detours to avoid German posts and patrols. Not content with that, when they had cleared the immediate district to their satisfaction, they started working further afield, extending their search as far even as Cambrai which was nearly thirty-five kilometres away. This meant several days far from home, journeys rendered possible only by the active help and hospitality of local patriots, often as not the curés of the villages, people who risked their liberty, even their lives, to promote the work that these girls were doing.

The arrival of parties at the château, always in the dark,

of course, and whenever possible on moonless nights, was heralded by a pull on a wire fence. Then the Princess would go out to meet them and question them in English. For the local people would sometimes mistake a German deserter for a British fugitive. One of the former had once actually got into the château! There they slept on the hospital beds at night, but hid their blankets etc. away during the day, and spent that in a shuttered room close to the *cachette*, the secret staircase in the medieval tower, into which they withdrew quickly on the alarm of approaching Germans. On one occasion a German officer expressed great archaeological interest in it at a time when Preston and Bushell were hiding inside! On another occasion sixteen men were thrust into it just before a party of Germans started to search the house while the Princess sat there, resentful at being disturbed, and calmly continued her embroidery. They did not find them, but they did find the wine cellar and took away most of it. 'When to my great relief the cart and escort left the grounds,' writes the Princess, 'I opened the panelling of the staircase, and the sixteen men emerged looking pale and frightened. They had heard the shouting, the guttural orders, and the knocking on the walls. They all thought their last hour had come.'

Meanwhile Prince Réginald had come to hear of, and got in touch with, Miss Cavell. 'She now offered to lodge any men we should send to her on the way to Holland, and arranged a code word with Réginald by which she would recognise our fugitives. They were to announce themselves as coming from Mr Yorc, the letters of our name reversed.' So when fugitives arrived at Bellignies there were three things that now had to be done. First they had to be disguised as civilians and, even if already disguised as such, often more suitably disguised so as not to arouse suspicion during the long tram journey into Brussels. Then they had to be photographed. This the Princess did with an old camera and a stock of large plates, which she happened to have, cut into small pieces with a glazier's diamond. Then they had to be provided with forged identity cards, on which their photographs were stuck, the forms for which were again obtained by the Prince through the Belgian clerk in the *Bureau de Population* in Mons who scrounged them while his German master was out in the lunch-hour. These, too, had to be stamped, and Derveau, the pharmacist in Mons, contrived a stamp to look very like the official German one and bearing the name of an imaginary commune. (Later these passes were provided by Capiau from the German office in Wasmes.) All was now ready for the men to move off, and when the coast was sufficiently clear of Germans they were guided into Mons on foot, and thence by tram into Brussels, by the Prince himself, by Mlle Thuliez when not otherwise engaged, by the Countess Jeanne de Belleville, or by some faithful servant of the family.

The two movements, the one in the Belgian Borinage and the other in the French Etapen, both with the same intent, i.e. helping Allied fugitives to escape, had now linked up through Miss Cavell in Brussels and its work continued uninterrupted until the axe fell on it at the end of July. All the important people in it were then arrested with the exception of the Prince who, when he heard of the arrest of Miss Cavell and Philippe Baucq, went straight to Brussels, first to see Maître Braun, a lawyer, and then to the Hôtel de Ville, in order to organise their defence at their trial. He also visited several houses where fugitives were in hiding, waiting to get to the frontier, in order to warn them; and also went to see and warn Ada Bodart, the Irish widow of a Belgian, who had been actively associated with him and Miss Cavell in hiding fugitives. When two Russians taken prisoner in the east escaped from a train that was carrying them to work behind the German lines in the west, the Prince had helped them to reach Brussels, and Mme Bodart had hidden them in her house along with three French soldiers and one British. Then Baucq had guided them to the frontier and the whole party had got away. Now she told him that her own son, a schoolboy, had just been arrested, and offered to go and warn some more fugitives in hiding near the Gare de Midi so that the Prince could catch his tram back to Mons. There the door was opened by a German policeman, and it was Ada Bodart who was arrested, not the Prince!

Prince Réginald returned to Bellignies that night to get another shock. Their close confederate, Herman Capiau, had also been arrested by the Germans, and Mme Capiau now implored the Prince to do all he could on her husband's behalf. So the Prince went back to Bellignies next day, but feeling that Bellignies was unsafe returned to Brussels. It was indeed. A few days later the Countess Jeanne de Belleville was arrested at her home, and the Germans then descended on the château at Bellignies demanding to know the where-abouts of Prince Réginald. The Princess got them off on a false scent. She succeeded in making them believe that he had gone to visit his estates at Solre to the south, and the Germans, divining that he was probably hiding in the woods, set off there. Not finding the Prince they arrested his head gamekeeper instead.

Meanwhile Prince Réginald was really staying in the house of friends, the Lichterveldere, in Brussels, and there a mysterious man came to see him. He proved to be a glazier, who worked for Philippe Baucq, and who, thanks to the connivance of the Belgian Governor of the prison of St Gille, M. Maron, carried a message from Baucq to the Prince. He was liable to be arrested any moment, it said, and if he got caught he would certainly be shot. He must now get away himself at all costs.

So Marie de Lichtervelde went to see a French nun of her acquaintance, the Superior of the Clinique de Linthout, and told her the whole story. On hearing it she at once agreed to take in the Prince as a patient under a false name. There he stayed until the wife of a sick German officer in the clinic started to ask awkward questions about the mysterious gentleman who kept himself so much to himself and spent all day in the garden! Some other place of hiding now had to be found, and the Prince moved to the humble abode in Brussels of the sister of the curé's housekeeper at Bellignies. Her husband was at the war, and the only other member of her household was a little maid-of-all-work of very low intelligence and most unlikely to talk. But every day it was becoming more urgent for the Prince to get away. The Germans had seized all photographs of him at Bellignies. These had been circulated to the police, and a high price set on his head.

'Marie de Lichtervelde now made attempt after attempt,' writes the Princess Marie de Croy, 'to get into touch with one of the many associations which had been working on the same lines as ours, but frequent arrests had dislocated all the services, and a reinforced watch on the roads, especially along the frontier, had made it much more difficult to get out of Belgium.' Eventually however Marie de Lichtervelde got into touch, through friends, with Henri Beyns, a Flemish working man living on the outskirts of Brussels. He was acting as *passeur* or guide to a nun who, under the name of Mlle Joséphine, was helping young Belgians to get out of the country and join the Army. For although priests, monks and nuns did not actively help fugitive soldiers to get out of the country, usually only hiding them, they did actively help young Belgians to get out, and it is to their efforts to which the Princess almost certainly refers when she speaks of 'many other associations working on the same lines as ours'. For the

o

Roman Catholic Church, led by Cardinal Mercier, Archbishop of Malines, was strongly anti-German. *Si tout le monde,* wrote Henri Beyns to Prince Réginald on March 7th, 1916, *faisait leur devoir comme les pauvres religieux et le clergé catholique qui travaillent nuit et jour pour notre chère patrie, cela irait dix fois mieux, mais, malheureusement, c'est justement la contraire avec quelques bourgeois et des mauvaises femmes, ils ne font que trahir et faire prendre les Belges qui font leur devoir.*

Before they could start, as the Prince could no longer use his German pass to get out of Brussels, he had to establish false identity of some kind. Fortunately he was found to resemble a young Belgian who had died recently in Holland, and a young woman undertook to accompany the Prince to the Hôtel de Ville and swear to his identity as René Desmet before a German official. They could now leave Brussels, and travelled by tram as far as Vilvorde, after which Beyns considered it unsafe to proceed except on foot. At Waechten all the bridges were guarded but, under cover of darkness, a friend of Beyns ferried them across the Dyle and they put up at his cottage for the night. Next day they were joined by a M. Maldeghen, and the three went on together through the woods of Westerloo to the Abbey of Tongerloo. There the monks hid them, while they waited several days in vain, and in increasing risk to their hosts, for a local guide with special knowledge of the frontier and of the disposition of German troops on it. Then they decided to go on to some people known to Beyns, a family 'always ready to run the risk of sheltering fugitives'. Eventually, sleeping in woods or haystacks by day and travelling only by night, they arrived at Baelen. 'These people were miserably poor but, without asking money, they were always prepared to take in anyone they knew to be in danger and share their potatoes, black bread, and chicory with them.'

At last, after further days of waiting, a local guide was

found who promised to get them across the canal by night, and appointed as a rendezvous a hut in a wood not far from the canal. There, when the Prince and his party reached it, they were held up by several men at the point of the pistol who, suspecting that they might be Germans in disguise, insisted on searching them for firearms and seeing their papers. Eventually they were satisfied that the Prince and his party were genuine. Eventually, too, the guide himself turned up, and they got ready to start. Beyns had provided himself with a length of rope and a canvas bag for their clothes. He also carried two packets of letters and some military documents. The Prince and M. Maldeghen, the only two strong swimmers, now swam across and tied the rope to a tree on the opposite bank so that the rest could pull themselves over. The guide came across first. Beyns followed with the bag containing their clothes, and the documents and letters. The rest started to follow, but when half had got across, the rope parted, and one man fell into the canal with a loud splash. Immediately the German post, only two hundred yards away up the canal, turned their searchlight in that direction and all were compelled to lie low, although they knew that one man who could not swim was struggling in the water, and that some of them were still on the wrong side of the canal without their clothes.

After a while Beyns crawled back to the bank, and lay for some time hidden in the rushes. But he could not see or hear anything, and before long their guide became nervous, and fearful of being caught by daylight, said they must push on. So they left the clothes belonging to the men who had not got across at a cottage—history does not relate what happened to them—and, their guide going on ahead, they started to 'feel their way' across marshy land in the dark. Crossing one dyke Beyns missed the plank and fell in, but hung on to his bag of papers, and the Prince managed to pull him out. In all they still had seven kilometres to go before they reached the frontier, and only when the day was breaking did they see soldiers sitting round a fire. Were they Dutch? Crawling up cautiously they listened. They were speaking Dutch! So they shouted and ran in, and were cordially received by the Dutch guard who provided them with a guide to the village. Thence they got a conveyance to the nearest station. There they got into a first-class carriage. This, in view of their appearance, excited a certain amount of comment, and at Rotterdam the police were surprised when an unshaven gentleman, dressed only in his trousers and a coat—the Prince had lost his underclothes in transit—maintained that he was on his way to the Hague to see his cousin the Prince de Ligne.

Beyns returned across the frontier into Belgium—but by what route and when I do not know—to continue the underground work in which he had been engaged in connection with an illicit postal service. This had started soon after the fall of Antwerp, and enabled Belgian soldiers fighting with the Allies on the Western Front to communicate with their relatives in German-occupied Belgium. Their letters were collected and taken to Holland, then carried across the frontier by Beyns and distributed all over Belgium. The replies were then collected, and carried back across the frontier by Beyns, whence they were sent to the Belgian Army fighting on the Western Front. Beyns carried eighty thousand letters across the frontier.

He was also engaged in a number of other underground activities. He carried information of military value across. He helped a number of other distinguished people besides Prince Réginald to escape; also helped many young men of military age to cross the frontier to enlist in the armed forces of the Allies, among them his own son who was killed fighting on the Western Front at the age of seventeen. He carried the first seventy-two numbers of *La Libre Belgique* across to be sent to the Belgian Government at Le Havre, and was involved in a scheme to blow up the bridge across the Meuse at Namur. For this purpose he carried thirty kilograms of dynamite across the frontier from Holland, and was given instructions as to how to do it. Indeed, all was set to do it, at a moment to coincide with an Allied offensive in the West, when he got caught. This was on June 27th, 1916, near Grebendenken, on his forty-eighth crossing of the frontier.

For three months he was kept in prison during which every effort was made to extract information out of him. But he refused to give anything away. Then he was tried by court martial, and sentenced to death. Again he was kept waiting, and after another three months this sentence was commuted to hard labour for life. Then after a second trial on a charge of conveying recruits to the enemy, he was sent to Rheinbach where he served his sentence until liberated by the Armistice. He was decorated both by the French and Belgian governments, and awarded the British Military Medal.

On the eve of going to press I received the following letter in reply to enquiries which I addressed to the monastery at Averbode. It is particularly interesting in relation to Chapter XI of Beaumont's story and belies my facile statement, made above, to the effect that the Church took little active part in helping fugitive soldiers to escape!

Translation:

> *Village Street 32,*
> *Ekeron.*
> *November 16th, 1966.*

Monsieur le Docteur,
    At the beginning of 1915 (I cannot remember the exact date), a Belgian soldier by the name of Petit, a native of Villerot in Hainaut,

arrived at the Abbey of Averbode. He had been charged with a mission by our Ministry of War at Le Havre. (The Belgian Government was at Le Havre.) They had learned that many British soldiers had been cut off from their units in the retreat from Charleroi and Mons and that some still managed to remain in hiding in the forest of Maubeuge. Petit was to collect them, and get them over into Holland, and it had been suggested to him to evacuate them through the Abbey of Averbode by way of which several people had already managed to escape. So our Reverend Father, the Abbé, now made me responsible for this business in collaboration with Petit. He, Petit, now got the soldiers together into small groups, guided them to Averbode, or sometimes into Brussels or into Louvain. There I took charge of them and made sure they got into Holland safely.

To do this I got into touch with guides on whose patriotism I could rely. They would let me know the night before when it would be propitious to start. For the whole country was thick with German patrols which became more and more numerous as one got near the frontier. Sometimes groups of fugitives would have to stay several days at the Abbey before they could start. When they did, the itinerary was always the same. From the Abbey they were guided cross country through fields and forests to Mol where lived our chief guide Eduard Vermeylen. There the men had to cross a bridge over the canal. This was always a particularly dangerous spot. Then, under cover of darkness they were guided across a second canal to Dessel, in the course of which they would have to get through electrified wire, and avoid German night patrols. On one occasion they had to stretch a rope across in haste and pull themselves over on a makeshift ferry. Once the canal was crossed the rest was easy. The Low Country was now only a quarter of an hour away.

The next day the guide brought me a note, given him by one of the soldiers, to prove that the party had really got into Holland and so get his reward. The parties usually numbered four or a few more, but I remember one party of as many as eighteen.

I remember the group you speak about in your letter. I think there was one Scotsman among them.[1] *I had got into the habit of giving each soldier, on his departure,* une médaille religieuse de Notre Dame du Sacré Cœur d'Averbode. *It was only later that I discovered how imprudent I had been. The Belgian soldier Petit returned to Holland with the last group, having accomplished his mission, and he wrote to me triumphantly to the effect that all the soldiers, about three hundred, had actually arrived in England.*

In 1919, when the war was over, I tried to contact some of these men we had helped. I had heard that the Colonel of their regiment was named Crawford, and I wrote and asked him to put a notice in the English papers. He replied that the English soldier was a casual forgetful chap and that he had not been able to get in touch with any of them. He invited me to go and see him at Anabank, Ayr, Scotland, to talk about those days, but I was never able to go.

That, Monsieur le Docteur, is some of the things I remember of that period. I hope they will interest you, and I will willingly give you, if I can, any further help you want.

Haute considération,

Frater Michael Appermans

Three hundred surprised me, and Petit may have exaggerated, but it is impossible to ascertain the facts. All that the *History of the War* has to say is that 'on Sept. 5th (1914) there were 20,000 missing, . . . but a large proportion rejoined their regiments later', and then adds, 'the official figures show a little over 15,000 killed, wounded and missing.' This was the price the Regular Army paid for one of the most gallant episodes in its history; against overwhelming odds the orderly retreat from Mons.

---

1. This is clearly Brother Michael's mistake. The one 'Scotsman among the English' was Beaumont. As the reader will remember, the rest were Irishmen.

Index

9